The Process of Magic

A Guide to How Magic Works

The Process of Magic:

A Guide to How Magic Works

Taylor Ellwood

Portland, Oregon

The Process of Magic: A Guide to How Magic Works

by Taylor Ellwood

Cover Art: Mark Reid

Editor: Kat Bailey

Layout: Taylor Ellwood

Set in Consolas and Book Antiqua

ME 0004

ISBN: 978-1720827306

A Magical Experiments Publication

http://www.magicalexperiments.com

Other Books by Taylor Ellwood

Pop Culture Magick

Pop Culture Magic 2.0

Pop Culture Magic Systems

Space/Time Magic

Space/Time Magic Foundations

Inner Alchemy

Manifesting Wealth

Magical Identity

The Book of Good Practices (With Bill Whitcomb)

Creating Magical Entities (With David Michael Cunningham & Amanda Wagener)

A Magical Life

Mystical Journeys

Magical Movements

Coming Soon

Alchemy of Life

Dedication

To all the students who took this class and to anyone who chooses to learn how and why magic works.

Table of Contents

Foreword

The Process of Magic was originally designed to be a 26 lesson class that people could take from me. I offered it as a class for a few years and each week a person would get an email with a lesson from me. Eventually I tried to make the Process of Magic into an evergreen online course that people could sign up for whenever they wanted, but that approach didn't work out very well. I debated whether I should go back to just occasionally offering the Process of Magic as a class, but I came to a couple key conclusions based on my experiences of trying to teach magic.

The first conclusion is that I don't like teaching magic. I don't like covering the same ground over and over again. The second conclusion I came to is that what I enjoy is doing magic and writing about what I'm doing and sharing it with others so they can do whatever they want to do with it. I'm much happier experimenting with magic and writing about it than I am teaching it to people.

So I decided I would turn the Process of Magic into a book, revise it a bit further and then publish it and let people get whatever they'll get from it. And some of that comes from the simple fact that I self-taught myself magic and have found that for the most part (with one exception), I've learned more from reading books and experimenting with the concepts and exercises in those books than I would from taking classes from the people writing those books. And I figure the same applies to me. You'll get more out of reading this book and experimenting with the exercises than what you'd get from me teaching you.

And like I said I've got some experiments to get back to, some other work I want to be doing. But I also want you to have this book. So here's the Process of Magic, reorganized and revised, and with some additional material I've come up with along the way that's relevant to what the Process of Magic is all about.

And what's the Process of Magic all about?

The Process of Magic is my take on how and why magic works. It's the gritty foundation that informs how magic works and how you can achieve consistent results. It's a systematic approach to magic that strips away the mythology, tradition, and every other religious trapping, and focuses instead on the technique and technology of magic. It's designed to teach you how to create your own workable system of magic, and make sure that you actually understand how and why magic works, so you can get consistent results.

It's also the closest I'll ever get to writing a 101 book on magic, but it's not a 101 book because I don't include a bunch of spells or rehash everything everyone else has already written about magic or anything else like that. And I'm assuming you have some experience at practicing magic, but that you also want to get better results than what you're getting. What it is…a comprehensive and analytical perspective on how magic works that pulls no punches when it comes to stripping away everything that's optional so you can get to the root of how magic works and take your magical practice to the next level.

A quick note about pronouns. I adopted to use the gender neutral pronoun of they for both singular and plural purposes.

Enjoy.

Taylor Ellwood
May 2018

Introduction

You're probably wondering (I imagine you're wondering), why is Taylor using the word process with magic. Afterall that has to be one of the most unmagical, clinical words, ever, and yet you're using it to describe how magic works. And you're right...the word process is not typically used in books on magic. The reason I've chosen to use it is as much a reflection of my background as a professional as it is because I apply process to my own magical work. But I've also chosen to use it because a process describes how something ought to work from start to finish and it's a lot easier to fix a broken process, because you know how it ought to work from start to finish.

So what is a process? A process is a defined set of actions that are used to produce consistent results. These actions can be diagrammed, analyzed, and tracked to determine if a result is being produced, or if something (or someone) needs to be changed in the process. The actions within the process can also be analyzed in terms of what is needed to perform the action, as well as being able to see the relationship one action has to another action. A process approach to magic allows you to track what actions work, and what components of those actions work, while also identifying weak links that can stop or subvert your magical work. A process approach to magic provides a holistic perspective of yourself as a person and magician, as well as of the actions you take.

I first began applying process to magic while I was working on my Ph.d in Literacy, Rhetoric, and Social Practice. While I never finished the Ph.D my exposure to social sciences and communication theory initiated me into process and this initiation was further refined by my years in technical writing. I developed a keen appreciation for being able to lay out a given magic technique and examine its components. I also discovered that such an approach allowed me to identify what didn't work for me, so that I could refine a given technique of magic and still produce effective results.

This perspective on magic runs counter to some of the established theories of magic, but those theories are weighed down by traditionalism as opposed to critical inquiry, which I have applied to magic. At the same time, I'd be remiss if I didn't mention William G. Gray. While I never had the privilege to meet this magician, his books on magic, particularly *Magical Ritual Methods* has influenced my own approach magic. Gray, much like myself, was able to analyze a given type of magical working and take it apart and explain it with an eye toward improving how it could be performed.

My approach to magic has always been a descriptive, as opposed to prescriptive, approach. Whenever people told me that Pop Culture Magic was just reinventing the wheel or tried to tell me that an experiment wouldn't work, it always made me question why they felt the need to discourage me. I came to two conclusions about that matter. First, the majority of books on magic are prescriptive. In other words, the books instruct people how to practice magic a very specific way and typically warn against experimentation or doing things differently. The second conclusion is that many magicians lack imagination and feel envious when someone else is creative about their process of magic. They feel a need to discourage such creativity to make up for their own inadequacies.

I prefer a descriptive approach to magic. A descriptive approach to magic favors the idea that any writing on magic is ultimately a description, but not a final authority, of magic. It encourages the practitioner to develop their own understanding of magic and further encourages an exploration of multiple disciplines and how they can applied to magical work. This descriptive approach is a theme you will find in all of my books and it has been purposely encouraged to combat what I consider to be ultimately stagnant ways of thinking and practicing magic.

I've defined process, so let's also define magic, with a caveat. The definition of magic I use in this introduction is primarily used to give us a foundation for terminology, but later in the book you will be asked to provide your own definition of magic, and that definition may differ from the one I provide here. And that is just fine if that's the case. For now, however, the definition of magic is: Magic is a technology that uses specific metaphysical and mundane actions to turn possibilities into specific realities, called results, which have a tangible impact on a person's life, in a way and manner that benefits the person. **Note:** This is not necessarily the definition of magic I subscribe to, but it is one I am using to create a discourse for this book.

The focus of this book is to present the process of magic as a method of analyzing magical techniques so that you can understand the underlying fundamental principles of how a given magical technique works, and then personalize that magical technique. This shouldn't be considered a magic 101 book, so much as it is an analysis of why magical techniques work, with an eye toward personalizing them. As such the focus of the book is to provide highly targeted information that explores particular concepts and techniques. The benefit of this is that each lesson allows you to fully explore a key component of the process of magic.

It is not required that you do daily work. I recognize that some people will read this book because they just want to read what I've put together. Others may take their time, which is fine. With that said, I do strongly encourage daily practice. I've found it to be beneficial not only for my magical work, but overall life quality, and I suspect you will as well.

If you are looking for someone to tell you how to practice magic, this book will not give you that. But if you are looking for a way to experiment with magic and improve your understanding of it as a process and practice in your life, this course will help you develop the necessary tools and insights to personalize your magical process and develop consistent and meaningful results in your life.

Lesson One: An Overview of the Process of Magic

Magic is a process. Strip away all the religious trappings, esoteric terminology, and ceremonial tools and what you have is a process that people use to turn possibility into reality. Understanding this process is all you really need to successfully practice magic. Everything else is icing on the cake, and yet that icing is the expression of the process of magic for each person.

Where most people get hung up with magic is that they mistake the icing for the actual cake. They focus on the candles, the incense, the oils, and frankly the image of magic, without really going deep and exploring the actual reality of magic. The icing isn't the cake, and the image of magic isn't the reality of magic.

Why use process?

I use the word process because a process is a mapped out activity that defines specific results as well as actions taken to achieve those results, and it also defines the relevant participants needed to execute those actions. A process approach to magic allows you to examine your activities and analyze what is working and what isn't working, as well as determine what you need to do to resolve the weak links in your magical process.

Such an approach allows you to understand how magic works, which in my opinion, is essential for being able to use it as a proactive force in your life.

In western occultism, the typical usage for magic is reactive. A problem occurs and you use magic to resolve the crisis. And if the result goes away, try again. You'll even have authors advocate that you don't need to know how magic works (makes me wonder why they're writing about it), so long as it does work. But with such an approach, inevitably magic won't work and you'll be left dealing with a problem that could've been resolved if you simply understand how magic works, and didn't treat it as a push button phenomenon.

A proactive approach to magical practice looks to resolve problems before they become problems. It puts the burden of responsibility on the magician to not merely be proficient in magical techniques, but also to be proficient in a skill that is essential for truly mastering magic: Know thyself magician. To know yourself is to know your place in your magical process. More importantly to know yourself allows you to recognize your weaknesses, both as a person, and magician, and start working toward resolving them before they become problems that cause undue drama in your life and the lives of others.

These lessons are not a spell book, but what you learn will help you understand spells and learn why they do or don't work, as well as how you can modify them to fit your personal approach to magic. Some people will argue that you shouldn't experiment or modify spells, but I think the most effective spells are ones that you've personalized to fit your understanding of the world. As you'll see, there are certain variables that need to be accounted for in order to develop an effective process of magic. These variables tend to be discounted by many magicians, but conversely they tend to be less successful in their magical work as a result.

Here is the process of magic without everything else attached

You: You are the most essential part of your magical process. Without you in the picture, magic wouldn't happen, at least as it pertains to your life. The very act of living your life brings you into situations that call for an action. Many people don't practice magic, either because they don't think it's a viable option or because they hold superstitious beliefs about it, but magic is a methodology for taking action to change your life. When we look at you, what we are looking at isn't just your sense of self or your reactions, but your identity. This includes your health, your relationship with your body, your familial and cultural values and beliefs, and much more. All of these aspects form a person with distinct needs and wants, which also inform how you approach magic. You may never fully know yourself, but knowing yourself is nonetheless an important part of your magical process. In fact it is the keystone to your foundation. Without you there would be no magic in your life.

Your Definition of Magic: The most fundamental principle of the process is the definition of magic that is applied to it. That definition is a description and explanation of magic and its place in your life. Many magicians will rely on the definition that someone else came up with for magic, most notably Aleister Crowley's definition, but I would urge you to develop your own definition of magic, instead of relying on someone else's. I've discussed definitions and their relationship to magic at some length in *Multi-Media Magic* and *Magical Identity*, and I'll discuss them again in one of the lessons to illustrate why it is useful to develop your own definitions instead of relying on someone else's.

Results: We are told not to lust for specific results, and yet if magic is to be effective, we need to know the specific result we are shooting for. This means we need to clearly define what it is we want our magical activity to achieve. Knowing your result doesn't mean you lust for it, but it does provide direction for the magical process you are engaged in and indicates whether or not your magical process is working. A result is the expression and embodiment of your magical process, and it is also an indicator of what you can improve on with your magical process. If you haven't achieved the specific result you wanted, then you need to look at your magical process and make changes to what you are doing. Keep in mind that even when you don't achieve the result you wanted, you've still gotten a result....it's just one that indicates that something isn't working the way you thought it would. A result, positive or negative, will always provide you information about your magical process and what you need to do to improve on it. I'll touch on this a lot more in a couple of later lessons.

What activities are you doing: A process is comprised of the activities you are doing to realize that process. Each process has steps that a person performs, so in planning your magical process out, it's a good idea to look at what steps you are taking. If there's a particular order to the steps, then arrange them in that order so that you can look at your process and/or zoom in on a specific step. Knowing the steps you will take to realize a process can help you answer several other questions.

Why are you doing it: You may be able to answer this question by looking at the desired result you want to achieve, but chances are that while a specific result will contain one reason why you are doing the magical process, it won't provide all the reasons. It's good to spend some thinking about why you need to do a particular magical process. What are your motivations for doing it? How will it help you improve your life (or the lives of others)? What need is doing this process fulfilling for you?

How does it work: How does your process work? Answering this question is essential to understanding what happens when it doesn't work as well as what you'll change about it. You should be able to describe in detail what every tool does, what every gesture or word contributes to your magical work. If you can't explain it, then why include it? Even the role of a deity or an entity should be something you can explain. How your process works, how the steps you do provide you the ability to turn a possibility into reality is something you should know. When you know how your process works, it will always work. And when you know how it works you can always improve on it.

Where/when: For some people this will be an important part of their magical process. They might choose to do magic at a particular time of day or week or month. I personally don't think it's that relevant, but remember what I said about your definition of magic. Your process of magic is one that is personalized. If the time of day and where you do something is relevant to your process then include it in your process.

Techniques: Your magical process is defined by the techniques that you use to execute your magical process. Invocation, evocation, enchantments, etc. are all examples of techniques.

There are some other variables you should consider that aren't traditionally covered in most occult books, but nonetheless should be considered because they are relevant to the practitioner. The practitioner is a key component of the magical process and if you don't consider these variables, then you ignore how you are influenced by them to your own detriment. The beliefs and values that a practitioner has is derived from these variables. Being able to examine these variables will help you understand how the magical process is allowing you to express those beliefs and values or determine if there is a conflict of interest. If there is a conflict of interest, it is suggested that the practitioner go back to the drawing board to build a magical process that accounts for these variables. So what are the variables? Read on, young (or old) padawan.

Culture: Your cultural background and interests will inform your magical process. What you identify as your culture is an influence that affects what magical forces you'll work with. If you're a Celtic reconstructionist, then you'll want to draw on that cultural information for your magical process. Or if you're like me and you find pop culture to be interesting, then you will want to use pop culture spirits as part of your magical work.

Ethics/Morals: If you follow an ethical code, then you will need to consider that code in your magical process. Likewise if you have particular morals that you follow, those will need to be considered. Trying to do a magical process that goes against your ethics or morals will always fail. If you're someone who tends to take a shades of grey approach to life, then you'll likely be able to find reasons that will justify doing the magical process, but I'd still look at that part of your process very carefully.

Ideology: Ideology is another factor to consider, particularly as it pertains to types of magic. If you identify as an anarchist, trying to do some form of money magic will likely be harder to pull off given how linked money is to the structures that the anarchist might oppose. Your ideology can also be a religious belief system and as such that particular system will need to be considered when performing magic.

Communication/Language/Symbols: Language and symbols are tools we use to frame and explain concepts and experiences, which includes magical concepts and experiences. The very fact that you are reading these words attests to how important language and symbols are. I'd argue that magic is another form of communication or at the very least that communication is a central function or activity of magical work.

Your Body: I mentioned your body above, in brief, but it's worth exploring in more depth. Your body is the single magical tool you absolutely need and can't do without. Your body also provides its own input to the communication that you do with people, and in my opinion magic. The tired cliche of your body being a temple is true to some extent. For purposes of your magical process your body is the embodiment of your identity and also they key mechanism for grounding possibilities into reality. If you didn't have a body you wouldn't exist, at least not in a corporeal form.

Exercise

Take each of the categories I've discussed above: Definitions, Ideology, How does it work, etc, and write about your practice of magic as it fits each of these categories. If a category doesn't seem to be relevant to your practice, explain why it isn't relevant and ask yourself what would be relevant instead.

Two Popular Misconceptions about Magic

"Watch with glittering eyes the whole world around you, because the greatest secrets are always hidden in the most unlikely places. Those who don't believe in magic will never find it." -Roald Dahl

There are two popular misconceptions about the practice of magic that occur, which can hinder useful inquiry and understanding of magical work.

The first popular misconception is special effects magic, the type seen on TV shows, video games, and movies, comics, and fantasy books. For example, Darth Vader using telekinesis to crush the throat of someone, or a sorcerer changing into a serpent or throwing a fireball, etc.

The second misconception is a belief that magic will solve all your problems, or as I call it the cure all approach. These popular misconceptions get in the way of what genuine magical work is about, and typically are sought after because a person desires a sense of power in their life.

Special effects magic looks impressive. Who wouldn't find it thrilling to throw a fireball or change their physical shape, or do something else equally impressive? I've yet to meet a magician who can perform special effects magic (without using special effects). If there were such people, I suspect the world would be a different place, though I can't help wondering how such power wouldn't be abused or worse end up like a comic book formula of endless battles and trite commentary.

There's also the principle of limitation to consider (more on this in a later lesson), specifically the understanding that force needs to be limited in order for form to be realized. In magical work, the achievement of form occurs when force is limited. Additionally, it is understood that when you work with magical energies you can only raise so much of that energy before you hit a limit, and/or have that limit imposed by the forces you are working with. Thus throwing a fireball, which would require a lot of force is not something that will be easily performed. In fact, when you account for the amount of energy needed to generate a fire ball, plus the amount of protection needed by the practitioner while handling said fireball, what you end up realizing is that it's not a very practical working. And if you mess it up, you'll either internally combust or burn your hands or do something else equally messy. The same applies to shape shifting and telekinetically handling objects or crushing people's throats. The physical demands, plus the amount of energy that needs to be raised to perform either feat is not something that is physically or magically possible. Special effects magic looks impressive and thrills lots of people, but a practical approach to magic acknowledges that the main focus of magic isn't to necessarily generate such physical demonstrations and also notes that such demonstrations may end up being more of a waste of energy than anything else.

Then we have the cure all misconception, which focuses on the idea that magic will solve all your problems. The sad fact is that while magic can be used to solve problems, most times it's used in that way, it is done so as a reaction and usually what is solved the symptom, but not the underlying issues that need to be examined by the magician. A proactive approach to utilizing magic to solve problems generally involves a fair amount of internal work and a willingness to own your dysfunctions and make changes that resolve those issues, with the understanding that such changes will also improve your life, and surprisingly enough decrease the number of times magic is needed to solve a problem.

There's also the fact that sometimes magic complicates issues more than it cures or resolves them. It shouldn't be surprising that many magicians end up complicating their lives when using magic to solve a problem. The problem might be solved, but not in the way they expected, and it may bring out underlying issues that need to be addressed (thus the need for internal work). A person who believes magic will solve all their problems needs to examine the level of responsibility they are willing to take to have those problems solved, because that level of responsibility is exactly what you'll be dealing with when you utilize magic as a cure all. There is no force that can solve your problems for you better than your own ability to take responsibility and deal with the problems head on. It can be hard work, but it is good work as well.

Two purposes for utilizing magic

"Magick is by one definition, if you will, the science of making things happen according to your desires in order to maximize control over one's life and immediate environment to create a universe that is perfecting in its kindness to you"
- Genesis P-orridge

The definition I've used above is a good one for describing one of the purposes that magic is used for. Indeed it's fair to say that it's descriptive of how most magicians approach magic. But it's not the only purpose. What should be clear however is that magic is a process of turning possibilities into reality, when this kind of definition is used. This definition focuses on **thaumaturgical** or practical magic. The purpose of this kind of magic is to create practical solutions for a person's life, or to create a universe that is perfect in its kindness towards you. How this occurs is through turning possibilities into reality, but to do that, there also needs to be an awareness as to how likely a possibility could become reality. The more likely a possibility can become reality, the easier it is to manifest that possibility through magic. The more unlikely, the more energy required.

Thus one of the reasons the wise magician marries mundane efforts to magical efforts to realize a practical goal. For example, if you want to use magic to find a job, you still have to go out and fill out applications, submit resumes, and get interviewed. The magic doesn't work in the absence of those activities. It enhances those activities and more specifically the favorable and desired outcome that results due to doing those activities. It's stacking the odds in your favor. If you don't do the mundane activities, it becomes harder to manifest the desired possibility. Many people, when realizing that magic works this way, seem surprised because they have believed in magic as a wave of the wand and everything appears. The reality is that magic is a process that interfaces with other processes. When you utilize magic you are accessing possibilities and discovering what it will take not only magically, but also mundanely to make it all happen.

Turning possibility into reality involves clearly understanding what the desired result is, as well as understanding how it will apply to your life. Many people take a reactive approach to utilizing practical magic, which means they'll employ it when they need to solve a problem. The proactive approach involves utilizing magic to make your life easier, but this also means doing a fair amount of internal work to understand and work with your issues. I think it's fair to say that there will always be some reactive use to magic, but if a magician can make the practical work be more proactive, they will find it much easier to manifest and keep desired results.

There is also **theurgical** magic, magic done for spiritual work. This type of magic differs from practical magic because the focus is not on obtaining practical results, but instead is focused on spiritual communion and the evolution of the magician. Theurgical work involves the attunement of the magician to spiritual energies and forces. It can also involve doing work for your community or environment that isn't necessarily for the benefit of yourself (as occurs in practical magic), but instead is part of the mission of your theurgical work. A fair amount of theurgical work is also internal work, in the sense that the magician needs to understand themselves well enough to not sabotage the theurgical work they are doing. Know thyself magician is a fundamental understanding of the necessity of self-awareness as it applies to the spiritual evolution of the magician and their spiritual mission.

Practical and spiritual magic can and does sometimes blend together, but in general I'd say they tend to be different focuses and paths. I'm more of a practical magician, with the majority of my work and experiments focused on obtaining results, but there is some work that is more theurgical in nature. Both purposes are equally valid forms of magical practice. Magic is less about the fantastic and much more about living life on your own terms. When you realize this, you also realize that living life on your terms is actually quite fantastic, not only in terms of joy, but also the recognition that many people do not live life on their own terms.

In future lessons we will cover the individual elements of the process of magic in detail. What's most important is that you recognize that there is a process of magic. Your process may differ from mine and that's ok. What's important is that you look at your magical practice from a process perspective so that you can assess what's working and what isn't working.

Lesson 2: You and Definitions of Magic

In the previous lesson, I mentioned that you are an integral part of your magical process. This probably seems like a self-evident statement, but it's worth exploring more carefully. When we make assumptions about given parts of the magical process we undermine that process, because we may miss out on details that could either sabotage or enhance our magical workings.

Your magical process begins and ends with you. What that means is that in order for magic to change your life, you have to play an essential role in that change. Even if someone else is doing magic for you, you still play a role in that magical process. But what does this really mean? You don't consist of just your conscious awareness. You is your identity. It's your cultural (and sub-cultural) values, your family heritage and beliefs, the physiology of your body and its impact on your life, your biases and prejudices, and your values and beliefs, based off experiences you've had. You sounds complex.

All of these factors that comprise you can have an effect on your magical work. And unless you've chosen to work with them actively, you may not even be aware of them and how they affect your magical process. In fact, I'd argue that what typically sabotages a magician is themself, especially if they haven't done internal work to examine their identity. This is why internal work is so important. A magician who is actively engaged in such work will sabotage themself much less frequently and also be less reactive to situations in general. Instead of using to magic reactively solve a problem, the magician will be proactive in their approach to life, minimizing problems while working toward specific goals that will improve their life and the lives of other people around them.

This isn't to say that you are trying to achieve enlightenment. But when you examine yourself as part of your magical process, it can be a good exercise to look at how you've used magic in your life. Has it been something you've employed when you've experienced a crisis or problem? Or are you using magic strictly for spiritual work? Or are you practicing magic to enhance how you plan your life and live it? There's no wrong answer, but the difference between a reactive and proactive approach to magic is significant, in the sense that it is an indicator of whether you are dictating the pace of your life or letting others dictate that pace. Nor is there anything wrong with practicing magic for strictly spiritual reasons, but it's also worth examining how magic might enhance your life.

Exercise

What is the primary purpose of your magical work? Has it been primarily proactive or reactive magic? Has it primarily been for spiritual or practical purposes?

Magic starts with you and knowing yourself is one of the most significant magical acts you can do and embody. As such it's worthwhile to invest in some program of internal work that helps you explore your identity and make changes to those beliefs and values that you may feel are getting the way of living your ideal life. In later lessons I'll discuss types of internal work you can do to work with your identity. What's most important at this point is that you recognize yourself as an active part of any given magical process you engage in. This recognition, in and of itself, will help you fine tune your magical process, for any magical work you do.

Your Definition of Magic

In *Multi-Media Magic* and *Magical Identity,* I've discussed definitions of magic extensively, in terms of looking at other people's definitions of magic and providing my own definition. However, I think it's important to examine YOUR definition of magic, and determine what it is and how you can use it. It's also important to understand what definitions are, in and of themselves, and why they can be potent tools for not only your magical practice, but your life.

At the root of any methodology, process, or practice there are definitions. Definitions are the root or the core of the process. They explain the need for the process as well as how that process fits into your life. Think of definitions as a concise statement of your beliefs and values. Those beliefs and values are integral to the success or lack thereof of your magical process. The definition embodies your understanding of those values and beliefs and their place in your life and your magical work.

Definitions are at the core of every magical process, and our ability to understand and change definitions is how we are able to use magic to turn possibility into reality. While many people think of definitions in terms of a dictionary or as a means of objectively describing the essence of something, definitions are not objective, but instead are based on subjective perspectives. We create some of the definitions we use each day, but many more of them are often created by other people, with their own agendas. Definitions can be thought of as a type of social knowledge that is used to create a shared understanding of the world, people, events, etc., as well as how all of these ought to be interpreted.

Definitions are central to shaping a person's identity because of how influential they are in shaping our social activities and perception of the overall world. To do effective internal work means being able to critically examine these definitions and determine if we really want to keep using them. Because definitions are based in part off of beliefs, it's worthwhile to look at the definitions we use and determine if those definitions are in our best interest or are holding us back. We can also think of definitions as a means of framing concepts in easily understandable terms. We use definitions to apply our understanding of concepts and experiences to the world around us, but also to the internal reality that comprises our identity.

For example, every person has definitions about finances and money. These definitions are usually learned from other family members, though in some cases people will learn them from books or other people who aren't family. These definitions shape how a person interacts with money, what they believe about their own financial abilities, spending habits, and other facets of their relationship with money and finances. And until those definitions are changed, the person can't make effective changes to how they handle finances, because those definitions inform the actions they will take. This also applies to every other area of life.

To truly change your life means you need to change the definitions that you either have created or believe in, which inform your perspective and actions in living your life. It's not as easy as it sounds, because that kind of change usually involves doing deep internal work to change your subconscious acceptance of the beliefs and definitions holding you back. It also involves examining cultural beliefs and ideologies that influence your definitions and perspectives, even when you think they don't. Because we can't discard our cultural assumptions and beliefs, we need to also remember that in working with our sense of identity, we are also working with cultural beliefs and values that are deeply embedded and will resist being changed. However, we can change our participation in the cultural concepts if we are willing to redefine ourselves and our understanding of the world.

What is essential to understand about definitions is that they ultimately are a means by which a person explains and understands the world, events, other people, etc. With that in mind, it's best to develop your own definitions than rely upon others, unless your reliance is a result of an informed choice. Remember that what definitions really do is describe the

functional relationship that something has with the world, which is powerful if we consider that such relationships can also be changed (and often are in various ways). When we understand that definitions are normative and prescriptive, we also begin to realize how much they can control our perspectives. We need to **choose carefully what definitions we really believe in,** as well as recognize that what gives a definition power on a cultural and community level is the consensual agreement that the definition has value to people using it.

On an internal level, a definition has power so long as an individual chooses to believe in what the definition represents. It's worth noting that a definition may not have personal meaning to an individual, but can still have significant meaning to a given community. As such, differing definitions can lead to people splitting from their communities in order to find other people who hold similar definitions. A good example of this is a child who discovers they are Pagan. While their parents might be Christian, their choice to become a Pagan will likely change the relationship they have with the world and their parents, as well as people with whom the child associates. When we choose our own definitions we empower ourselves, because we are consciously choosing how we will define our lives and our behaviors. We are advocating for our own interests and values instead of subscribing to the interests and values of others.

The relationship between definitions and magic is simple: How we choose to define our experiences shapes our perspectives and our reasons for doing an action, mundane or magical. By recognizing this principle we can critically examine the definitions we rely on to make sense of the world and determine if they still have validity, or if they are holding us back from truly realizing the life we want to live. When we critically examine our definitions, we also examine our actions, which includes magical actions. Suddenly the choice to do a magical act to handle a situation is viewed differently, when we realize that it is done as a reaction to a situation, as opposed to being a strategic, conscious choice. For many magicians, magic is used as a problem solver, a way of reacting to problems that occur in the life of the magician. There's certainly nothing wrong with using magic to resolve a problem, but if the tendency is to rely on magic whenever a problem comes up, it can be problematic if the magician is only using magic to solve the problem as opposed to taking the time to critically examine his/her own role in causing the problem.

Part of how we examine our own roles in the problems we experience involves looking at our definitions and asking how they contribute to the problem. If you find yourself experiencing similar problems on a regular basis, chances are that on some level you are contributing to those problems occurring in your life. Nothing happens in a vacuum, and while it is true that you have limited control of the environment around you, it's also true that you have the option of controlling yourself. You also have control over how you choose to react to a situation, even if the situation itself is out of your control. To truly learn to control yourself means taking the time to understand how your perceptions of yourself and the world around you contribute to the situations you are in.

It's very important to recognize that the reason people use definitions reflects the values they express in their lives. Magic is another means for expressing those values, and when we combine a sophisticated and conscious awareness of definitions with magical work, the result we get are magical processes that are targeted toward creating specific and lasting change in our lives. Effective magic is less about being esoteric and more about **being able to apply significant change to one's life** so that they can have a more meaningful life.

Before doing a magical act, take time to look at why you want to do the magical act. Ask yourself how you are defining the situation and your response to it. By taking the time to consider these issues carefully, you can determine if your definition is contributing to the situation in a negative or positive manner. Make changes to your definition, so that you can change your identity. Once that's done, then do the magic to effect the world around you. It's only after you've made changes to your identity and your definitions about the situation that you can effectively apply magic to solve the problem. And you may find that you don't need to change anything, because you've already changed the definition and that has provided everything you needed.

Our definitions affect the magical acts we do. I've said it above and I'm saying it again to emphasize how important it is to dig in underneath the surface to learn why we are choosing to solve a problem through magic. Your definitions are the keys to the door of your identity. They tell you what you really identify with, as well as show you how to change that. You can't really do effective magic until you take control of your definitions and start changing them into definitions you've chosen for yourself. Until you do that, you are living on someone else's definitions, letting that someone else define and shape your identity, and for that matter your actions and choices. To truly wake up is to stop reacting and start asking what really defines your actions and choices. Is it you or something else?

What sabotages a person's magical working is usually the definition of magic...or to be more particular, it's the fact that you are doing a process that is not aligned with your internal beliefs and values. For any magical work to be successful in both the short and long term, it necessarily must align with the beliefs and values that you live your life by. If the magical working doesn't align with your values and beliefs, you will, on a subconscious level, find a way to sabotage your results in order to bring you back into alignment with your beliefs and values. However, you can change your beliefs and values, though it will take some work.

Your definition of magic will vary to some degree by situation and circumstance. In other words, you may find that your magical work is more effective for certain situations or problems and less effective for others. If you find that to be the case, it's time to examine your beliefs and values about a particular situation. They may not be the problem in your process, but usually they are a contributing factor. If you want to change your approach to a given area of life, you have to first change the beliefs and values that inform your perspective and actions. This is true regardless of whether you are employing magic or some other methodology to promote change in your life.

There are two basic types of magical work: internal and external magic. All magical processes can be grouped into either of these types. Internal magic is magic directed toward working on the self. This includes internal work, which is done to work through psychological and emotional issues, but also includes magic that focuses on the physical health of the body. Internal magic is useful for examining and changing beliefs and values that you have. External magic is focused on influencing the environment around the person, in order to produce a physical change. Typically, in Western magic, the majority of the focus is on external magic and obtaining results.

Your definition of magic, however, is one that is based on your beliefs and values and thus fits into internal magic. I think it's a good practice to do internal work to clarify your beliefs and values, before doing external magical work to resolve a problem. By having a clear understanding of your internal motivations, you can then perform an act of external magic. You want to have a good balance between internal and external magic. Too much internal work ultimately leads to a lot of navel gazing and little action being taken, but too much focus on external magical work can find you reacting to situations without really resolving the core issues that cause the situations to occur.

A good definition of magic is one that helps you understand how and when to employ magic in your life. You can do rituals a few hours a day, but not really make anything come out of it, if you don't have a definition of magic that supports what you are striving to achieve and if you don't really understand how those rituals fit into living the life you want to embody.

There is one cautionary statement I wish to offer and it has to do with using other people's definitions of magic. While it might be tempting to simply rely on Crowley's definition of magic (a lot of magicians do just that) or someone else's definition, it is the lazy magician who does so! If you can't take the time to examine the core of your methodology and processes, you likely aren't making the time to find out who you really are, or what you really want. A personalized definition is one that is arrived at through experience and self-awareness. It doesn't just describe magic, but it also describes the person's relationship with magic and your understanding of how to apply it to your life. Draw on other definitions for inspiration, but learn to develop your own as well. It will provide you more insight into how magic works, and also who you are as a person than relying on someone else's definition ever will.

Exercise

What is your definition of magic? Why are you using that definition of magic? Does it accurately describe how magic fits into your life or how you want it to fit into your life? Does that definition fit your core values and beliefs?

Lesson 3: Results, Change and their respective roles within magic

We always get results. We don't always get the results we want, but we get results. In magic, we are told not to lust for results, but conversely we are also told to look to results to prove that magic is effective, and that our magical process works. The reason we are told not to lust for results is because if we do, the obsession we put toward that desired result removes the obtainment of it from us. And I think there's some truth to that reason. I've known people who've become obsessive and let that obsession consume them, which has stopped them from recognizing opportunities that were coming their way. The more they've focused on the result, the further away it seems to be, tantalizing, dancing just out of range of being realized. They put so much effort into getting it that they end up keeping it from themselves. You've probably had this occur or know someone who it's occurred to. You can feel the frustration pouring off of them, because they can't get the result they want and they obsess about it.

In fact, I remember one such incident myself. When I lived in Seattle, I wanted to get a job as a technical writer. I put together my resume and I sent it out and I did some magic to speed the job hunt along. In the meantime I also landed a job cleaning houses, which in all honesty was the most degrading job I've ever worked at. I met up with a friend who I sent the resume to. She'd passed the resume onto a recruiter and the recruiter told her that she wouldn't even interview me, because the energy that she got off the resume was so depressed and unhappy that she didn't want anything to do with it. I was so obsessed with getting a technical writing job and so pissed off that I was in a job I hated. I was getting a result, but it was a result that indicated that there was something wrong with my process: My attitude. Once I changed my attitude, I started getting calls for positions. Soon after, I left the cleaning job behind and landed a technical writing position at Boeing.

As you can see in the example above, I did a magical working and I achieved a result. It wasn't the desired result, because I was obsessed with the desired result and ended up putting a lot of negative emotional energy toward it, in a way that sabotaged my magical process. But I did get a result. Any magical working you do produces a result, but what is most important to understand is that the result is ultimately only an indicator if your magical process works. The current fixation on results in Western Magic is a result of approaching magic strictly for self-gain. Such an approach is a reactive approach, based more on trying to satisfy wants and desires. This isn't to say that doing magic for that purpose is bad. Sometimes you need to do magic for self-gain and for practical, mundane reasons that involve making your life easier. But when we focus so much on results we ignore their role in the process of magic.

A result is like a sign on the road. It indicates if you are going the right or wrong way, but just reaching the result doesn't mean your magical process ends. A result brings with it consequences, for example. The consequences of getting a job as a technical writer in Seattle involved a long commute, working five days a week, a paycheck, etc. Some of the consequences are good and some are not so good, but all of them ripple out from your result and influence your life, which in turn influences your magical practice. Even when you practice magic with more of a spiritual focus, you still deal with results. Every magical act has a result and the result indicates if you are working the magical process successfully or if it isn't working in quite the way you thought. I see a result as an excellent way to diagnose your magical process, because no matter what result you get, it will tell you if your magical process is working or needs to be refined.

You need to know what result you want to achieve in order to create a magical process that will (ideally) get you that result. It is also helpful to be as specific as possible in defining and describing the result. A vague description of a desired result isn't very helpful or useful. For example, if your result is: "I want a job", that's fairly vague. It doesn't provide much focus for the magic and as such won't be much of an indicator as to whether your magical process is working. On the other hand if you state: "I want a teaching position, where I make at least 60,000 a year and have opportunities to advance in my school district.", then you have a more specific result that you are aiming for. You might need to define it further, but even as is, this specific result will indicate if your magical process is working. The failure to achieve a specific outcome that you've defined, for example, will show that something needed to be changed in your process. The more specificity you use to define your result, the better you'll able to define and refine your magical process.

Developing a specific result allows you to develop a specific magical process to help you achieve that result. Here are some questions to keep in mind as you define your result:

1. What is the result I want?

2. What are additional details I can include to make the result more specific? Additional details should include anything that you would consider important or helpful.

3. Why do I want this result? How will it benefit my life to achieve this result? Does this result create a healthier, happier lifestyle for myself? What is the impact of the result on other people? Am I comfortable with the consequences?

4. Is there any part of this desired result that I don't agree with or feel resistant toward? If there is part of me that feels resistant to it, why do I feel that way?

5. How will I feel once the result is achieved? What will I do with the result?

All of these questions can help you not only develop a specific result, but also determine if it's a result that you can achieve. If you discover that there is resistance toward the result, it's a good idea to spend some time looking at the reasons for that resistance, to determine if the result is something you really want. Otherwise that resistance will become the element that sabotages your magical process. Below is an example of a specific result I created in January 2012, as part of a magical process I used to create business.

I will have five new clients by October 2012. Having five new clients will provide five new revenue streams and more financial stability. I will work with these clients for approximately 6 months to a year, or possibly longer, depending on the level of coaching they need. Once I am finished working with these clients, they will have achieved their own goals and will give me testimonials as well as referring other potential clients to me. I'll also stay in touch with them to check in on their progress and be available to offer services, if they need additional help.

In April 2012 I had five clients that fit the criteria I've established above. I could easily foresee working with each of them for at least six months. At that point I refined the result so that I can get more clients by October of 2012, using the combination of a business magic working and mundane work I was doing to develop my business.

This is actually a good example to draw on, because when we talk about using results to indicate if our magical process is working, it's worthwhile to note that a successful result can be useful for indicating a need to refine your magical process. While a failure definitely indicates a need to refine and change your magical process, there can be a tendency to rest on your laurels when you've achieved a successful result. I say why settle for achieving that result, if you know you can achieve an even better result? While it's certainly nice to have five new clients for my business, I wanted more than just five new clients. The achievement of that specific result indicates that the magic is working, but it also indicates that I could be more ambitious with my magical work, as well as the other work I am doing. My point in saying all of this is simple: Don't settle for the success of achieving a result, if you know that you want more success. Use the success to motivate you to do even better! At the same time, if the success is exactly what you want it, then enjoy it and don't push for more if that's not what you want.

And one other thing. Success is temporary. Yes I got 5 new clients back then, but eventually I helped and they moved on and I discovered I didn't like having so many clients at a time, which caused me to reevaluate what I wanted to do with my business, but that's a story for another time.

As you can see results are an integral part of your magical process. I'd argue that defining your result is the first step of your magical process. You need to have an end goal in mind for what you are doing. Once you have the end goal defined, THEN you can do the internal work to check in and see if you are in alignment with that result. From there you do the magical and mundane work needed to achieve the result.

Exercise

What's a recent result you obtained? How did you define that result? What could you have done to define it in further detail? How, if at all, have you made results part of your magical workings?

The Role of Change in the Process of Magic

In the first lesson, I didn't include change in my descriptors of the process of magic. I purposely chose not to. Change is one of those understated elements of magic that is part of any and everyone's process. That's probably why it's understated, because change of some kind or another is expected to occur when you do magical work. Consequently there is a tendency to not really discuss change in context to magic. But I'd argue that change is an essential part of magic, and something to explore, because there are different types of change.

In magical work, the magician is looking to create purposeful, conscious changes via magic. However not all change is purposeful or conscious change. Change can come from any vector, and some of that change is not going to be in your favor. Some of that change will be random, simple chance, and some of it is change directed by other people trying to make their own way in the world. All of that change is present within the field of probabilities the magician manipulates. The difference is that the magician has magic on their side, which gives the change they induces an edge over the other changes that are available. But change isn't something you can take for granted. Your magical process isn't just about causing change to occur, but also about factoring in other changes that could potentially occur so that you can adjust your process as needed.

Change needs to be examined in conjunction with results. Your result is the explicit indicator that change has occurred. Without a result you wouldn't really know if your magic worked. But change is more than just a result. Change is a transformation of the environment around you and within you. Respecting that aspect of the magical process is really important for understanding how magic work. There needs to be a change built into your process. Magic is a causative agent of change, and the employment of it is a signal that you want to bring change into your life. But it's also worth noting that even though you might get a specific result, you might also get other changes that are connected to the result, but weren't necessarily desired. This occurs, not because of the magic, but because of a lack of specificity about the result, or because specific consequences are triggered when a specific result occurs. How we deal with those changes is just as important as the magical process. Indeed, those changes may prompt more magical work on our parts as a way of addressing them.

Change is a constant in our lives. We change moment to moment, but intentional change is something a person chooses to create, and that's what makes magic distinct. It's a methodology used to produce intentional changes. When we recognize that change is intentional, then perhaps we consider it more carefully, recognizing that what it brings isn't just a result, but also the consequences that come with that result.

As such, when change occurs that isn't something the magician has purposely started, the way to approach this change isn't to try and deny it. You'd have better success with trying to stop the ocean from coming to the shore. Rather you must the accept change, but with an understanding that you work with it, and find opportunity in it. The magician who can accept change in general is one who can adapt to it, and adapt it to suit their purposes and methodologies. The acceptance of change is what allows you to master it. Your acceptance of it is an acceptance that it will always happen, but that it needn't control your life more than you allow it to.

For the purposes of your magical process, it's useful to meditate on change and how you can accept it and make it part of your magical process so that it fuels the work you do and allows you achieve the optimum results. Remember that change is a force and as such it is also inspiration and direction and movement. Use that movement in your magical work and you will have the momentum of the universe on your side.

Lesson 4: Why, What, Where, When, and How: The Anatomy of your Process

Your magical process initially starts when you recognize that you need a result to address a problem or bring about a change in your life or that you need a result that is focused on helping someone else or the environment around you. Ideally you have defined the result you need as specifically as possible. Now you need to construct a process of magic that will help you achieve that result. To do that you need to address specific questions that will help you understand the context of the magical work you are doing. Addressing the context allows you to identify variables that could affect your magical working in either a positive or negative manner. Optimally the identification of these variables will allow you to adapt your magical process so that you can capitalize on them to help you achieve the best possible outcome.

Why

Why are you doing this magical working? Why does this result matter so much? These are useful questions to ask yourself as you begin to construct a process. These questions answer what the underlying motivation is for doing a magical working. Unless you understand your motivation for why you are doing what you've chosen to do, there is a chance that your magical working won't succeed. You need to know why you are doing this working, and why this result matters so that you can be sure that all of you is in agreement about obtaining this result. If there is even a small part of you that disagrees with this working, that part of you will find a way to sabotage your working or sabotage the result, after you've obtained it. There's nothing more frustrating than doing something and not succeeding, because some part of you chose to sabotage your efforts.

Beyond examining your motives, asking why addresses the core of the magical working itself in the sense that if causes you to evaluate the importance of the result. Motivation is part of evaluating that importance, but when you choose to do a magical working you are stating that what you are working toward is something that is significantly important. Why else do the magical work unless it's something that NEEDS to occur. Understanding the role of need in magic is essential for getting your process to work.

What

What magical techniques or practices will you choose to utilize to help you achieve your result? What mundane activities will you do to support and sustain your magical work? These are useful questions to ask because it allows you to start framing your process with the actions you will take to accomplish it. A magical working ideally is supported by some form of mundane action, with the understanding that such an action creates a vector or path of least resistance for the magic to work through. As such it's important to include the mundane actions and even to examine how you can create a connection between your mundane and magical activities so that the mundane activities provide a source of power for the magical activities. In my experience, mundane activities that fuel your magical work make it that much more likely that your desired result will occur. The mundane activities demonstrate the commitment that you have toward achieving your goal and serve as a valuable way to fuel your magical working.

Certain magical activities will be more useful, dependent on the result you want to achieve, as well as how you want to achieve it, and what technique will provide the best emotional resolution for you. For example, it can be useful to work with magical entities in situations where they can perform specific actions that you can't perform. On the other hand, an enchantment can be just as effective because you are using it to directly influence the outcome of a particular situation. We'll discuss magical techniques and when to use them in more detail in later lessons.

Another consideration to take into account is what you will use to power your magical working. I've already mentioned using the effort you put into mundane actions as one source of power, but another source of power could be emotions that you feel toward the situation or drawing on the power of a deity, if you are working with one to resolve the situation. Knowing what you will draw on to fuel your magical working is an important part of how you'll determine what techniques to draw on.

Finally, it's also important to consider what magical tools (if any) you'll be using. While this might be answered by the technique you've chosen, that's not always the case, especially if you don't rely on traditional tools. Part of what determines what tools you use is how you've learned magic. If you have a ceremonial background then using ceremonial tools and garb could be an important part of how you prepare to do magic.

Where

Where will you do the ritual? Is there a specific space better suited for doing magical activities, and if so why? Sacred space, which is an integral part of magical work isn't just set up by creating a magical circle. It is set up by associating a specific space with your magical work. Whether that space is a specific room devoted to magical work, or a place that a person goes to, to do magical work, such a space is made sacred by intentionally choosing to associate that space with your magical work. Repeated work in such a space makes it an amplifier of your magical work.

On the other hand, there is something to be said for also being able to do magical work, on the fly, in any given space. In such a case, a space is made sacred by the person's ability to slip into an altered state of mind that enables them to create an association with the space that makes it sacred for the duration of the working. The reason this can occur is based on a person's understanding of space and how it relates to their identity. I cover this in depth in *Magical Identity*, but a brief explanation is warranted here.

Space is one of those elements that continues to fascinate me, especially when I look at how people use space to situate and express their own identity. I came to this perspective through the anthropological work of Edward T. Hall and Rudolf Laban's perspectives on space and movement. The occupation of space whether with objects or with politics or spirituality is something that occurs on a regular basis. Whether we realize it or not we are always creating difference versions of space in our homes, cars, work places, and other places through the intentions we bring into those space. The spaces we inhabit also act as mirrors for our identity. We embody our identity in those spaces, by how we choose to decorate them, what we put into the spaces that denotes our interests, and even what we tolerate within our space that we might not want, but put up with. We create a space that is the demonstration of us, and the things that interest us. We create spaces that can even provide insight into our internal mind and how organized or chaotic is, or even the state of our emotions.

Now apply this to magic. Magic is about changing a space. It changes a space by turning possibility into reality. Space changes, becomes a different space when a possibility is brought into reality. Space is changed by time, with the understanding that time is what brings possibility into reality, while space provides the necessary anchor for reality to exist in. A person is their own space. Space acts on space and in turn is acted on by space. The person expresses their space in the external space, but that same space also shapes the person's identity. When a person performs an act of magic they are inviting in both time, and specific defined spaces to modify the current space they inhabit, both in terms of identity, and in terms of circumstances the person is in. The very modification of space is an invitation for change in your life. Magic is part of how you make that change occur, but sometimes it can also be as simple as actually cleaning up a space and making it into something new that better suits who you want to be and how you show up.

Space is an event, person, place, or thing. A noun if we want to get grammatical, but what that really means is that space is more than just the experience of the person. It is the totality of the environment, the person's role in that environment, as well as what is done to modify the environment. Think of it as a Temporary Autonomous Zone (T.A.Z.) that Hakim Bey writes about it. Space is the creation of a particular reality and the fusion of that reality in a larger space that we can call the world or universe or whatever else. Where is important because it isn't just a physical space we occupy. It is a metaphysical space we embody in the physical space in order to bring possibility into reality and make changes that make our lives better (it is hoped). Understanding that helps us understand that space is something experienced through a variety of mediums, all of which can help us create the desired space we want to achieve and manifest in our lives.

When

Timing is everything. When will you do your magical act? Is there a specific time of Day or Night? Is your ritual timed to specific moments when something needs to be done? Is there a specific planetary hour you need to do your working during, or a moon phase that is relevant to the work you are doing? That's one way to look at time. It's a rhythmic sense of time based on cycles of time that include not only the cycle of a day or week, but also the cycle of the seasons and planetary movements. It's a planned approach to time that focuses on capitalizing on the right moment of time in order to do specific magical work.

Another way to look at time is: Time is an essential part of how a magical act occurs. When something will occur is an element that goes unstated the majority of the time, but is needed, or why do magic in the first place? You want a result and you usually want it within a specific period of time. When will the result be manifested? Is there a specific time it needs to occur by? What will happen if it isn't manifested in that time? Are there specific events that need to occur before the result can be manifested and if so is timing important for those events? Examining time, from this perspective, shows that timing could mean everything to your magical process. Understanding the role of time in your working is important in order to effectively use it in the execution of your process.

Time is action. You need time to exist in order for something to change. Magic couldn't occur if time didn't exist. Time is the measurement and progression of change. Time is the rhythm and movement of magic expressed in the world, moving the world to its own beat.

The perception of time, if nothing else, is how people make sense of and organize the events and information of their lives into coherent units of expression that can be accessed via memory. So when you think of when, think also of time as a necessary medium that provides a frame of reference that allows change to come into your life.

How

How will the magic work? Do you understand how it will work? While what tells you the technique you'll use, how demonstrates that you understand how the technique will work. If you don't understand how the magic works, chances are it won't work. How involves understanding the underlying principles of magic, and how those principles are executed in the magical work you do. Once you understand how magic works, you can make it work for you every time, under any circumstance. The need for tools and props goes away because you realize those tools and props are just things you use to put yourself into the right space to access the principles of magic. We've discussed some of those principles already, and we'll discuss them in further detail, but for now consider this: Magic operates on specific rules (or laws), but how those rules are executed or acted upon is up to the magician. A magician with sufficient imagination shouldn't have any problem shedding the ceremonial tools and robes or any other props, if need be. They understand that the true value of the props is that the magician can use them to shift into the right space to perform magic, but that same space can be accessed at any time, under any circumstance by simply knowing the rules and using them to your advantage.

I suspect that one of the reasons the current occult movement has become full of so many disenchanted magicians is because they've all bought into the psycholigization of magic, which argues it's all in your head and that you don't need to know how magic works. Consequently magic doesn't work so well and they become disenchanted because the spiritual dimension of it has been taken out of the equation. Let me just say there is always a spiritual dimension to magic and that the entities you work with are by no means just voices in your head. If they are, you might want to get checked out by a shrink.

Knowing how magic work entails accepting and understanding that there is a spiritual dimension to magic and that the rules of magic are based in part on that spiritual dimension as well as being based in possibility and specifically how possibility brought into reality. Ignoring the spiritual dimension of magic is a mistake made because many magicians have bought into a postmodern perspective of magic which focuses on utilizing magic for material gain. While there's nothing wrong with working toward your material success in life, the lack of any other motivation tends to be disspiriting and ultimately nihilistic. At some point material success just becomes a distraction that can never sate the uneasy realization that there has to be more to life than materialism.

There is more to life, but it involves accepting a spiritual dimension that includes the realization that we are connected to each other and everything else in this world on a far more intimate level than we realize. The rhythm of that connection is life and the changing of the rhythm is magic. Knowing this helps us to understand that what we're really dealing with, when it comes to magic, is patterns. When you can look around you and see the pattern and rhythm of life and feel it flow through you, then you have truly experienced magic and you have started to understand how it works and how to make the rules work for you.

If you want to understand how magic works, you need to consider that it's an experience and that the experience of magic involves a principle of connection, or created causality. How magic works: You create causality to make it work. That causality has to make sense to you, even if it doesn't make sense to anyone else. As long as it makes sense to you and it produces consistent results, then your magic works. As long as you can make causality fit the rules or make the rules fit your causality something will happen. The experience of that is something words can't fully convey, but you feel and know it when you perform a magical working and feel reality change to fit the possibility you've brought into existence.

Here's the real secret for how magic works. As long as you embody your magical working, i.e. tie it to the physical expression of your essence, then you've provided the desired result a connection to reality and you convey that connection through every action you take to make that desired result into a reality. It exists within you and is manifested externally to you through your actions that bring it into reality as an expression of your identity and your place within the universe.

Need vs. Desire: Which makes your process work better?

One of the words I see often in correlation to magic is desire. Desire is a powerful word and it can be a powerful motivator. What someone desires can move that person and cause that person to move whatever they needs to, in order to experience that desire. But I think if I were to really identify what I consider to be truly effective for powering your magical work...its need. Need is something you have to have. It's something so essential to your being, you can't live without it.

Desire can become need, but not all desires are needs. Many desires are things we want to have, but if push comes to shove we can do without. But need is something you can't do without. It defines the core of your existence. It motivates you to take action and do something to address it. It is something that nags at you, bothers you, drives you until you do something about it.

There are healthy and unhealthy needs. An addiction is an unhealthy need that can eventually consume you unless you get it under control. When you can transition an addiction from a need into a desire, you've started to de-fang it. It still has power, but it doesn't quite define you in the same way. Ultimately you have to do a lot of internal work as well as change your behavior to really change the addiction. A healthy need is something you need for survival, but you keep it moderated. For example, you need to eat food to stay alive. Being a glutton, on the other hand, is an unhealthy version of that need and not surprisingly there are consequences associated with it.

When you feel need, you know have to act. A desire is always a maybe, something to have, but not essential to your life. A Need is something that you have to have in order to live. And in magic, a need will always trump a want. People put more of themselves into a need than they do into something that's a want. Thus it's always useful to look at what the underlying motivation of a magical working is. Is there a need or a desire? How far will you go to realize the result you want to achieve? If you can inject a sense of need into your magical workings, it will not only help with the magic, it'll motivate you to take the necessary actions to make changes that help your magical process along.

Exercise

Take each type of question above and apply it to the last magical working you did. Is there an underlying process? Were there any parts of the process that didn't work? If so, why? How has doing this exercise helped your understanding of your practice of magic? And when you do your next magical process be sure to record your process.

How does need fit into your magical practice? What makes it relevant or non-relevant?

Lesson 5: Culture, Ideology, Ethics/morals and their place in the Magical Process

Each of these topics (culture, ideology and ethics/morals) are linked to each other and as such should be considered in relationship to each other, in order to illustrate their respective influences on the magical process. A magical working doesn't occur in a vacuum. There is the problem which necessitates the need for the magical working and there are the results and consequences which occur because the magical act is done. In the background are the values and beliefs a person has, which create the definition of magic used to explain why magic will or won't work.

Part of that background, however, is also based on culture, ideology and the ethics/morals a person has or doesn't have. Despite the fervent wishes of Wiccans that a person harms none with a magical working, there are many people who are quite capable of harming others through magic. This is because magic itself is not a moral or ethical force. It's important to know this in order to also understand why a magical process will or won't work. It's equally as important to understand how culture and ideology influence what a person is capable of doing. And with that we also need to understand the role of family and how even that can have an effect on your magical process.

American culture has been sold on the myth of the rugged individual, but the truth is that your average person is far more influenced by culture, ideology, and other such influences than s/he is willing to admit. Recognizing the influences of these forces allows us to situate our magical process into a context that can help us use these influences to effectively work magic.

Context is key in magic, and pretty much anything else in life. Context is what provides a measure of understanding and conversely an awareness of the limitations of what we understand. Every magical act you do has contexts you may not even be aware of, simply because magic, for the most part, doesn't just affect you. It has an effect on other people as well. For example, if you do magic to help you find a job, one of the contexts that you may not be aware of is that you've used it to give yourself an advantage over other people also hunting for a job. The recognition of that context can affect your magical work, in terms of how you choose to handle the context. For the most part, we learn to take such context in stride because we recognize that the employment of magic is done in part to put the odds in our favor, but it doesn't mean we should ignore the context in which our workings occur, or how those workings can affect other people.

We also shouldn't ignore what our cultural, ethical, moral, ideological, etc. backgrounds have to offer in terms of context. You might feel perfectly comfortable doing job magic, until you consider it from a moral context that makes you question how it is affecting other people. That kind of realization can derail your magical process unless you are able to make peace with it in a way that makes you feel comfortable with your choices. This level of awareness is a necessary part of cultivating a successful magical process.

Culture

When I talk about culture, I'm not merely referring to the culture you grow up in, but also to subcultures, and/or cultures you choose to adopt or appropriate from. Subcultures are niched groups or communities of people that place a particular importance on the subject of interest that brings them together. For example the occult community is a subculture. The Goth community is also a subculture. A person can belong to more than one subculture at the same time and may even find that there is a lot of overlap between the subcultures.

Culture, in general, is the overall unifying culture in which a person lives. For example, I live in the United States, and would associate myself with the overall culture that could be described as U.S. culture. A person who lives in Canada or Mexico will be part of a different culture. However we shouldn't assume that just because you're part of a nation that you're part of the culture. The Tibetans and Uyghur's live in China, but definitely have their own cultures, which are distinct from Chinese culture. While nations can help define a culture that a person is part of, it's also fair to say that ethnicity can also do the same, as is evident in any country where you have a diverse ethnic population. It's possible to belong to two cultures. You can belong to an ethnic culture and still identify with the national culture around you, but that identification occurs at a cross roads of the ethnic culture and the national culture and it can be tricky to navigate, as over identification with one culture or the other can result in an exclusion from one. There is the additional pressure of maintaining a distinct ethnic cultural identity when the national culture is bent on homogenizing other cultures.

Culture can be thought of as the values and beliefs of your community, as expressed through your lifestyle, behavior, and who you surround yourself with. There is always some level of identification with other people around you and it occurs partially through material goods and through behavior. The saying "keeping up with the Jones" is an example of how a cultural lifestyle centered around material goods can create a set of values that's focused on material acquisition. Status symbols such as a car or a house are examples of culture making itself known in what people choose to acquire and in the perception of how they will be judged by people around them.

Behaviors are another way culture is expressed. Your level of etiquette or manners is an example of how people study behavior in order to create a cultural code of conduct that helps people either fit in or be excluded for not demonstrating the proper behavior. Even words such as "please" and "thank you" are cultural constructs used to set up expectations of how people will act in public and private settings.

Who you surround yourself with is also used to indicate the kind of culture (or subculture) you belong to. The various cliques in high schools are an example, but you find it outside of institutional settings as well. The various labels we use for different people such as geek, hippie, entrepreneur have positive and negative cultural values associated with them. None of this might seem to matter, yet if you look at who you associate with you'll find people who dress similar to you, act similar to you, have similar values around material goods as you, etc. It's the flow of culture and it's something all of us must respect because it's part of our identity.

There are cases where people will adopt another culture. In some cases this adoption is legitimate. For example, people involved in reconstructionist movements are attempting to reconnect with the cultural heritage of past cultures. They will do everything they can to research the culture via academia, but also via magical work, in order to reconstruct it within their own lives and magical practices. They try to replicate those cultural practices in their lives. On the other hand, there are also people who will try to appropriate the practices of a contemporary culture. One example is the case where some people will appropriate Native American beliefs and practices and then pass themselves off as neo-shamans. Cultural appropriation is generally frowned on for the reason that it not only appropriates a cultural heritage, but it also distorts that cultural heritage for the person's own ends. At the same time, learning about the spiritual practices of other cultures is not necessarily a bad thing. You can learn a lot and expand your experience of the world. It's also hard to really say where cultural appropriation begins or ends. Is your choice to learn a Tibetan meditation cultural appropriation? Perhaps, but perhaps not. It's a gray area. I'll admit that I've chosen to learn a variety of spiritual practices that are outside of my culture and that I practice them on a regular basis, as well as write about them. If that makes me a cultural appropriator, then it probably applies to many other people I know.

The cultural filters we grow up with play a role in our beliefs and values, and even as we question these filters and explore what it means to belong to a particular culture, we can never fully escape the culture we are living in, unless we move somewhere else and adopt that culture. Even then, there will still be habits and behaviors that originate from the original culture. Culture is something ingrained within us, in ways we may never fully realize, simply because it affects us on so many different levels of our identity.

Culture is never static. It is always changing and this is evident in the cultural artifacts that are produced. Music, television, social media, etc., are mediums of cultural transmission and cultural artifacts that convey culture to all people who use those mediums. Some cultural artifacts are shared across cultures, though if you aren't from the native culture that the artifact originated from, there will be certain subtle details you won't get. Cultural artifacts are excellent magical tools and even frames for magical ritual because they provide structures that help us situate our experiences into concepts we can relate to, and use in our lives. Every tool, every action, will have some kind of cultural significance to the magician.

This is why it is important to draw on cultural influences that you can readily identify with. What will work for one person, may not work for another. For example, I personally wouldn't draw on ancient Greek or Celtic cultures, because I feel no resonance with them. Other people will however, especially if they've taken time to research those cultures and connect with the relevant deities and spirits. With that said, if you've never lived in a culture, no matter how much you might adopt it, you'll never know it the way people native to the culture will. None of us will ever really know what ancient Greek culture was like, because we've never lived in that culture and no one speaks ancient Greek. So even though a Greek Reconstructionist can make a connection to the Greek gods, they must also recognize that the cultural context that they know those gods is in part based on the contemporary culture they live in.

For a lot of my magical work, I've chosen to draw on pop culture, because it's contemporary culture that I can identify with. This doesn't necessarily make it superior to working with ancient cultural constructs, but because I'm immersed in the culture, I can understand those cultural constructs from a much more experiential perspective. They are a part of my life on a daily basis, in the background, as well as in activities I'm involved in. This is important to consider, simply because by living in a culture you understand it and are immersed in it and as such can access the cultural resources with a degree of understanding that can be taken for granted because you live in the culture. It's just my opinion, but I think ancient cultures are often romanticized while contemporary culture is looked down upon, but contemporary culture and its various artifacts has a lot to offer to the magician who chooses to draw on it. Regardless of what cultural resources you draw, it is important to recognize that culture influences your values and beliefs and also influences your understanding of magic in general. Nothing ever occurs outside the context of culture.

Ideology

When I think of ideology, I tend to associate it with political and economic movements, though it could also be associated with social, religious, and moral movements. I also think that ideology can extend across cultural boundaries. For example, Democracy and Communism are political ideologies that aren't culture specific and are shared across numerous countries. However democracy and communism also have moral, religious, social, and economic dimensions to their respective ideologies that inform how people think of and act toward those respective dimensions. While ideologies are not culture specific, interpretations of them can be culture specific, and often are. An ideological movement can also be thought of as an applied philosophy that directs peoples' actions as those actions pertain to their lifestyle choices and what they vote for.

Magic fits into ideology in the sense that ideology is another background influence that can motivate the need for change and inform the success of a change. However, it's worth noting that ideological changes are driven toward changing the political and social landscape of a culture toward values and beliefs associated with the ideology. This means that the change that is sought is applied to a larger spectrum than just bringing change to your life. Thus, for example, we see the far right Republican movement bolstered by the prayers of Christians. In the United States the Tea Party is a further extension of an ideological movement that is seeking to change the underpinning values of the Republican party in order to better represent the conservative views of the people who belong to the Tea Party. There can be magic in all of that, in the sense that a magical working can tap into the focus of the other people to work toward making changes in the ideological system...but do it carefully and remember the French revolution and all other revolutions. They start and end in blood and many times the leaders of the revolution are among the sacrificed.

In my opinion, it's important to acknowledge your ideological beliefs and how they can inform your magical work, as it applies to your life. I think trying to impose your ideology on other people is not wise to do. Many people will do it, but one has to ask why it is so important to make people agree with you? The reality is you can never achieve full consensus when you try to force it on people, either magically or mundanely. In my opinion, when people try to force their ideologies or beliefs on other people they are really trying to validate their own belief. They may feel insecure about what they believe, or they might have questions about it, but instead of actually doing the necessary internal work to validate themselves, they try to find validation by getting other people to agree with them. Christianity, in particular, stands out as an example, as many Christians have made it their personal mission to try and convert people to their beliefs, regardless of whether those people actually want to learn about the Christian religion.

Ethics/morals

Ethics are a code of behavior that is applied to professional activities. Different professions will have ethical codes that are applied to situations and define what the right and wrong choices are. Ethics provide guidelines that can help a person in a professional setting. Obviously there are also ethics in magical organizations and groups. The Wiccan rede is perhaps the most famous example, though with most magical organizations you'll find ethical codes that explain how the magician should behave toward other members of the organization as well as consequences. In fact, what's most notable about ethical codes is that they outline the consequences for what will happen if you violate the ethical code. The magician who adopts an ethical code has to consider carefully the oaths s/he swears, as well as the consequences for breaking those oaths. Following an ethical code will constrain some of the magical work you can do, provided you are sincere in following the code. And if you aren't, then you have to decide if the consequences are worth dealing with.

Ethical codes can affect your magical process simply in terms of narrowing the potential magic you can do to resolve a situation. This isn't necessarily a bad thing, as the choice to follow an ethical code shows a commitment and discipline that is essential to excelling at magical work. The very choice to live by an ethical code is one that has to be considered carefully, as it is one you would put into practice every day. If it's not something you can implement into your daily life, it's better to not adopt it.

Morals are personal codes of conduct, and are another expression of the values and beliefs that informs a person's definition of magic. Morals are the expression of your values and beliefs in your life. A moral code is not necessarily an absolute code, but it is a code that provides personal guidelines for your choices. It's different from an ethical code, because it's a self-imposed code. No one else is providing you guidance or expecting you to follow the code. A moral code is something you've chosen for yourself as a way to direct your life. You might even consider it a calling of sorts.

I'll admit that my moral code tends toward a gray view of the world. I take a situational approach to life, and as such apply my magic in a similar manner. Your mileage may vary. What's important is that you honor your moral code in your magical work as going against it can actually sabotage your magical process.

Exercise

Question: What cultures and sub-cultures do you identify with? What makes you part of those cultures?

Question: How do the cultures and sub-cultures you are part of influence your magical practice? How, if at all, do you apply those cultural influences to your magical practice?

Question: What are the ideologies that are part of your life? Do these ideologies apply to your magical practice and if so, how?
Question: What ethical code, if any, do you follow? How does it impact your magical work? If you don't follow an ethical code, why have you chosen not to? How does that impact your magical work?

Question: What is your moral compass? How does that it affect your magical practice?

Conclusion

Your cultural background and affiliations, ideology, and ethical/moral code are all influences that inform your values and beliefs. Spending some time exploring these influences can tell you a lot about your sense of self and can also help you understand your magical process better. To some degree or another, all of these factors influence your understanding of the world and your place within it. If you don't consciously explore these factors you may find that these factors undermine the efficacy of your magical work. By consciously exploring these issues, you can determine where they fit into your life, and how much influence they should really have on your magic and life.

Lesson 6: Connection and its role in the magical process

Connection is an integral principle of the process of magic. Understanding how a magical act connects a possibility to reality is something that a magician needs to know in order to effectively practice magic. Connection establishes the causal nature of magic, even if that nature isn't readily apparent to outside observers. Connection establishes, for the magician, the actual route that the magical work will take. What I mean by route is not even so much the process itself, but rather the magician's understanding of the process, as well as their understanding of how everything else relevant to the magical act fits into the process.

Connection also demonstrates the magician's understanding of what they are connecting with. For example, if you are doing an invocation to a deity, fundamentally you are trying to connect with the deity. That connection between yourself and the deity is shaped by what you know about the deity, on an intellectual, emotional, and belief level. It's not enough to read about a deity or do an occasional ritual to a deity if you want a genuine connection with it. A genuine connection is something that occurs on the level of your identity. You and the deity connect in a way that demonstrates a shared recognition of each other and the role that each of you plays in your respective existences. Your connection is an affirmation of that recognition and the power it has in your life, as well as how you apply that power to your life.

In fact, connection isn't just an awareness of the connection, but also an awareness of how it applies to your life. The connection you make to a deity, a specific result, a person, or anything else always has an application to your life. The manifestation of a possibility into reality occurs through the application of the connection to your life. When you make a connection to the possibility you are inviting it into your life, and at the same time using the act of connection to define how it will apply and appear in your life.

A connection is made partially through the meaning a person reads or imbues into the various elements that comprise the magical process and the situation the magical process is being used to resolve. A person's interpretation, although subjective, is powerful because it is how they make sense of the world and their place in it, as well as making sense of the situation, and the ideal resolution of the situation. Thus the magician understands that meaning itself is a tool, one that is used to explain and rationalize why the magical act is being done, while also being used to imprint that meaning on reality, so that it is easier to manifest desired possibilities into reality.

A recent example comes to mind: I was doing a banishing ritual, where I was banishing the meaning or emotional influence that some people had over me. I made sigils for each person, which were derived from their names, and even came up with a vocal pronunciation of their names. By imbuing my emotions about these people into the sigils and pronunciation of the names, I was able to create a connection between myself and the ritual actions I was doing, while also using those same ritual actions to change the connection I have with the people. I needed to put some meaning into each action I took if I wanted to create a connection between that action, myself, and the world at large. So when I lit the lighter and burned the sigils, I was also burning the emotional influences those people had in my life, and returning that energy to them. But for that to occur, I had to understand and know that there was a connection to my burning of the sigils and my disconnection from certain people in my life. I had to understand how that connection applied to the ritual working, so that I could then use it to perform the magical work.

This is what makes connection such an important magical principle. I'd argue that it's the most important principle, because it is the demonstration of your comprehension of how magic is supposed to affect you and the world. Without that comprehension, we can't do magic. Ask any person who practices magic how they think magic affects the world or how it works and they'll include some thoughts on how connection plays a role in magical work.

A connection is also partially defined by the actions a person takes to realize the connection. In other words a person needs to perform some kind of activity in order to fully demonstrate the validity of the connection, and establish that the connection will manifest the possibility the magician wants to realize. That activity will not only establish the validity of the connection, but also imprint it on the magician, and on reality.

Thus the actions you take in a ritual are really designed to demonstrate and imprint the connection between magic and reality. In the example, I used above I discussed how using a lighter to burn the sigils was part of the banishing ritual. That was just one action in the ritual. Here's the ritual in its entirety:

I developed sigils based off the names of the people I wanted to banish from my life. I took their names, got rid of repeating letters and turned the rest of the letters into a sigil. I wrote the sigils on pieces of paper. Afterwards, I vomited the negative emotions and energy I felt toward them on to the sigil papers. I didn't physically vomit, but rather made the motion of vomiting and allowed the sensation of the emotions to go out of my body and onto the paper. I then took a lighter and burned the sigils in a little cauldron. Afterwards I took the cauldron to the edge of my driveway and asked the elementals to scatter the ashes and recycle the energy into something good for the environment.

That's the description. Here's how the principle of connection relates to this process of magic. The first connection occurs when I takes the names of the people and turn them into sigils that represent who they are. When I vomit the negative feelings and energy onto each piece of paper, I am connecting that energy to those people, through the sigils that represent them. The act of vomiting also releases my connection to those feelings and energy. When I light the sigils on fire, I am burning those people from my life as well as turning the energy and feelings I have into ash, fully disconnecting myself from those people. I take the ashes to the edge of my driveway, signifying in that action that I am disconnecting anything about these people my life and anything related to my life. When I ask the elementals to scatter the ashes and recycle the energy, the connection to the act of banishment is fully realized by removing the ashes from my presence, and by taking the energy and turning it into something else that is not connected to those people. As you can see the various actions have some form of connection occurring, including the connection I make to the overall purpose of the ritual, which is to banish these people from my life.

What makes a good connection?

A good connection is something you can draw on as a source of power for your magical working. For example, your emotions can be part of what helps you make meaning and connects you to an event. But a connection doesn't just have to be emotional. A connection can also be tied to an archetypal force or role. For example, if you are a teacher, then your profession could be used as an inspiration for connection. To do this, you would develop a list of attributes that you'd consider to be important to the profession of teaching. If you found that you were lacking in some of those attributes, you might look to other teachers or pop culture references to teachers as potential sources to work with. You'd draw on those resources to create an archetype of a teacher, an idealized teacher if you will. The ritual you'd develop would involve invoking the idealized teacher and getting advice from him/her on how to improve your teaching skills.

Whenever you wanted to work with this idealized teacher, you might use a physical object to call him/her forth, such as a pen, or an icon of a teacher. That object would serve as a connector or aligner between you and the idealized teacher. You can also use existing deities or pop culture icons for the same purpose, but you have to be careful because you may end up drawing on negative attributes that you don't want, but nonetheless are part of the god or pop culture icon you are using.

A connection will always be something that has meaning to you. The meaning you associate with emotions, a role, or anything else is what makes any given person, event, thing, etc., into a connection. Your magical work frames your connection into a specific context that allows you to use that connection in support of your magical work. The connection will also always be related to the situation you are applying magic to. The connection needs to be relevant to that situation in order to make it effective for helping to resolve the situation. If it's not relevant, you'll have difficulty creating a connection because it won't make sense to you. Fundamentally a connection must make sense in order to be a good connection. Even if the logic only makes sense to you, it has to have some form of logical causality in your mind so that you can make the connection between what you are doing, what the magic is doing, and the manifestation of the result.

Exercise

Examine the last magical act you did to achieve specific results. What were the connections you drew on? What role did they play in the magical working and how did you identify their relevance? Explain why connection is a fundamental part of those workings.

Lesson 7: Function and its role in the process of magic

A function, in and of itself, describes a specific action that is supposed to occur within a process as well as why it occurs in the process in way it does. Function, in magic, also speaks to how spiritual entities are supposed to behave. For example, angels are defined by the functions they perform. Those functions are the actions the angels perform, as well as their area of responsibility, but in another sense the function is also the soul of the angel. This understanding of function can be applied to other "types" of spiritual entities as well.

When we consider function in relationship to process, what we discover is that function is what moves process along. A process that isn't working is usually not working because specific functions of the process aren't being activated or don't work the way they should. Without the right functions in place, a process fizzles. So how do you make sure you have the right functions in place? First you have to understand the process and where those functions fit into the process. For example if lighting a candle is a function in your magical process, what is it that function does? How does that function contribute to the process and move it along? What happens if that particular function isn't activated?

Likewise if you are working with an entity, it's worthwhile to consider how you are interacting with the function it embodies. That entity can't go against its function, so you pretty much need to be in alignment with that function. There's some wiggle room in my experience, but that wiggle room has more to do with interpretation of the function than actually getting around it. This is why it's important to be selective about what entity you'll work with, or if you're creating one be very specific about the function it's supposed to embody.

Although function sounds restrictive, it really isn't if you understand it. The given functions are restricted in terms of what they do, but where the magic really happens is when you combine multiple functions into a sequence that creates your process and produces a result. If you understand how each functions work off each other, then you can plan for which functions you'll use and optimize your magical working. One of the ways I like to optimize my workings is to thoroughly explore the functions I'm using to see what they can and can't do. Then I know where and when to apply them in whatever magical work I'm doing. This understanding of function makes it easier to find problems in the process as well and then fix those problems. A lot of times it boils down to: "This function doesn't work in relationship to this other function."

This probably comes across as a mechanistic approach to magic, but I don't think it is. If anything I feel that it helps me appreciate magic on a much deeper level because I can understand how and why it works and know what to change in order to improve on what I'm doing. I like that and at the same time it gives me a deep appreciation for the wonder of magic because it never ceases to cause me to feel wonder to see a process come together and produce a specific result.

Function is a lot like conjunction junction in magic

I wrote a blog post about function and its role in magic. In it I defined function: "A function, in and of itself, describes a specific action that is supposed to occur within a process as well as why it occurs in the process in way it does." I also explained that function, as it relates to spirits, describes the essence of those spirits and what they are supposed to do. Some of the responses I got to the post asked me to go into a deeper explanation of function and how it's supposed to work in magic and that got me to thinking about function and what came up initially as a way to explain function is the old school house rock tune "Conjunction Function, What's your function?" If you've never watched it, you should watch it because it's just that awesome. If you watch that video, it actually explains the concept of function quite nicely, but I'm still going to explain it in my own way as well.

The first thing I'd note about functions is that to some degree they are subjective. You use a function to describe an action and how it ought to work. Functions can also be likened to the attributes you associate with a component of magic, again with the understanding that the attribute, as a function, is describing how the component ought to work or how it ought represent a principle of magic.

The second thing I'd note about a function is that it's a connector. Functions are specific actions, which when executed lead to other functions which perform specific actions and so and so forth...get the picture? Basically a function connects to another function when executed properly. And if it isn't executed properly nothing happens. Usually when a function isn't executed properly it's because the people doing it don't understand why they are doing it or don't have a clear understanding of the principles involved. In my experience, to make a function, you have to understand why you are doing what you are doing and understand the principles involved. That lack of understanding translates into what you are doing and sabotages the working. Let's provide a specific example or two that helps demonstrate function.

One of my workings involved invoking Vinea, a Goetic Daimon. I was doing this invocation to make initial contact with him so that I can do further work with him in the future. Here's what happened. Step one: I briefly look over his name and sigil, to memorize the sigil and to make sure I know how to pronounce his name. The functions at work in this step are memorization (which will lead to another function) and Pronunciation (which will lead to another function). Both of these functions are the foundational functions used to set up the initial ground work of the invocation. Each function performs a specific action. Memorization imprints the sigil into my mind to be recalled when I need it, while pronunciation allows me to learn how to say the name for when I do my invocation chant.

Step 2: I lay down and get comfortable with my head against a pillow. I close my eyes and visualize the sigil, and mentally I say Vinea's name three times. The functions at work in this step are relaxation, visualization, and mental chanting of the name. Relaxation performs the action of getting you into a space where you aren't focused on your body so you can actually focus mentally and spiritually on connecting with the entity. Visualization performs the action of recalling the sigil and using it as a visual marker to focus on connecting with the entity. The mental chanting performs the action of building up your energy, while also creating an auditory link between you and the entity. Think of it as providing a path to connect you and the entity to each other.

Step 3: I whisper Vinea's name three times, then I say it louder 3 times, louder again 3 times, then I shout it 3 times. While saying his name, the sigil turns into a shape that is representative of him. The functions at work in this step are sonic chanting and visualization. Sonic chanting as a function builds on the initial auditory link you created with the mental chanting. It increases the resonance of the connection, establishing a way for the entity's energy to connect with yours through the pronunciation of the name. The visualization as function builds off the previous use, but in this case is also an indicator that the entity is connecting because he's choosing to appear to you in place of the sigil.

Step 4: I commune with Vinea. We essentially have a conversation which involves an exchange of images and words, as well as coming to an agreement (if we can) of how we'll work together and what we'll do for each other. The function in this step is the communion. It's a function that occurs on both ends and requires both parties to participate.

Step 5: Assuming an agreement is made I follow through on my end by doing agreed upon actions and Vinea follows through on his end. I won't spell out the functions here because this step occurs after the invocation has happened, but I mention it as an example of how functions lead into other functions past the actual working.

So as you can see functions are a lot like conjunction junction. They make connections. One function leads to another, which leads to another, and everything is pull together to produce a process that works. That process makes the magic happen, as long as you understand the functions and what they ought to do or rewrite them to work the way you think they ought to work (but that's another post altogether).

How you can Rewrite Function in Magic

Now we're going to explore how to rewrite a function in a magical process. When a process of magic doesn't work the way you expected it to, then you need to examine the functions of that process and likely rewrite them. A function is really the description of the action and how it ought to work. It is your understand of that action and how it executes a principle of magic in order to fulfill the process. Thus what you are rewriting or changing with the function is your understanding of that action and how it ought to work.

It's important to recognize the distinction of rewriting a function based on description as opposed to action. The action performed may change as a result of how we change the description, but we are changing the description so that we understand how the action works and can accordingly perform it to realize the process. When a process doesn't work, it's usually because the magician doesn't fully understand what is happening. That lack of understanding allows for variables in your magical process that can change what happens. In a sense, what understanding does is define the path of possibility and lock it in, so understanding is not only important in terms of knowing why actions occur and how magical principles inform those actions, but it is also important in terms of locking out unneeded variables and possibilities.

When you rewrite a function, you first examine it in terms of what ought to happen and ask why the action didn't happen the way it ought to have. What you'll likely discover is that the function doesn't connect to the next function in a way that is understandable. We humans need to know how something connects in order to fully accept that it will connect. And this mean that the connection needs to be logical or rational. It could be irrational, but it needs to make sense and if it doesn't make sense what that demonstrates is a lack of understanding of what the function is supposed to do and how what occurs fits in with everything else happening in your magical process.

Once you discover what the issue is, you need to rewrite the function. This involves changing what occurs when the function is executed so that it connects to other functions and makes sense to you when doing so. What this reveals to us is just how important it is for a given magical process to make sense to us. If it doesn't fully make sense, some part of us will reject it and that is what will truly sabotage the magical working. This isn't a matter of psychology, as much as it is a matter of comprehension. The way we comprehend the world and our own actions necessarily informs the magical work we do. To neglect that or assume it doesn't matter is to reject a crucial element of the magical work: Ourselves and how we execute the magical work through the functions we perform and our understanding of those functions. I don't think this aspect of magic is discussed enough or if it is, it's fashionably written off as being psychological, but I'd argue it's not psychological. It is a recognition that the magician is at the core of the magical process, and that their understanding of that process and the functions of the process is a key part of what makes the magical process work. They may understand the process and functions in different ways, spiritual, psychological, informational, etc., but however you categorize the understanding what matters is that they can connect the process to the result in a manner that makes sense and enables him/her to execute the process and manifest the magic into change that transforms reality.

Lesson 8: The Aesthetics of Magic

The other day an acquaintance emailed me and asked me what I thought about sigils. What the person wanted to know is if I thought chaos magic style sigils were an effective form of magic. I'll admit to being surprised by the question, because I've generally found the work, but then I read a bit further and I recognized why sigils hadn't worked for the person. The person explained that the sigils didn't look magical.

The issue was an aesthetic one. And it's an important issue actually, because if you look at the practice of magic in general there is an Aesthetic aspect to it that shows up across various systems and traditions, and yet isn't overtly acknowledged or recognized for the most part.

Let's define the word Aesthetic. Aesthetic is a set of principles that underline and guide the work of a particular artist or artistic movement. It's also the appreciation of beauty.

So what's that have to do with the practice of magic?

If we look at a given magical working from a design perspective, we see the aesthetic principle of magic show up. The design perspective is concerned with the trappings of magic and what trappings are needed in order for the magical working to happen. For example, what tools you will use, what clothes you will wear, but also how you will get your conscious and unconscious self to align and buy into the magical working.

This is why some people need incense and candles when they do magic. Aesthetically the incense and candles creates the right design that allows the person to fully commit to the magical working, because they've created a space that *is* magical.

Now what's important to remember is that not everyone's aesthetic is the same. For example, I don't need incense or candles to do magic. My aesthetic of magic is fairly minimalistic in some ways...yet there is an aesthetic that informs the magical work that I'm doing.

I would also say that your aesthetic for a given magical act can actually differ depending on what the magical working is. For instance if I'm doing a chant to evoke an archangel...that chant and the correspondences in it will be the aesthetic that makes the working come together. On the other hand, a painting of a sigil doesn't need a chant, but does need the paints and the experience of paint, and so that becomes the aesthetic.

Now that's just my take on the aesthetic of magic and as you know I'll all about personalizing magic, so to me it makes sense to take an approach to the aesthetics of magic that personalizes them according to the magical working that you'll be doing...but a reasonable question to ask is if a person should develop a universal standard of aesthetics that they apply to their magical practice.

The answer to that question is that it depends on the person. For that matter it also depends on what spiritual system or tradition they are engaged in, because a given system or tradition of magic has its own aesthetic of magic that informs the design of the rituals and how people should show up. You can question that aesthetic and modify it, but you also have to consider whether said modification will be welcomed by the other people in that system or tradition.

If you're developing your own system than you can create a codified aesthetic for that system. That codified aesthetic is essentially your brand and it describes how your magic should be designed and why that design will play a role in the magical work you do, as well as the interactions you have with the spirits that are part of your system. This codified aesthetic should also have some input from your spirits, because of course they'll have their own expectations and correspondences that need to be considering when you're doing a working with them.

How does the Aesthetics of Magic connect to the Process of Magic?

I think the aesthetics of magic offers another angle that you can use to help you understand your process of magic and why something is or isn't working. And recognizing that your magical practice should be experienced a certain way helps you to appreciate how you design your magical works, as well as what is essential and what is optional in those workings. Additionally, there's something to be said for simply appreciating the qualities of a magical working that make it magical.

So let's explore how we can apply the aesthetics of magic as a form of inquiry into your magical practice.

First and foremost let me ask you this question: What makes a magical working magic? In other words, what do you need to have in that working to make the working magical to you?

To go back to the example of the person who didn't feel sigils were an effective magical working, the main problem was that the sigils didn't "look magical". The experience of drawing the sigils, charging them and firing them didn't work because the person couldn't get into the experience. What would need to change is that the person would have to figure out how to aesthetically design the sigils so that they looked magical (and thus were magical).

At the heart of the aesthetic of magic is experience, specifically the experience you create and have when doing the magical working. A magical working is made effective when the experience of doing the working takes over your conscious mind, aligns it with your subconscious and puts you into an altered space of reality where you can work with the desired possibilities you want to manifest.

So really this boils down to what is essential to your experience of magic and how you create that experience. So here's a few questions for you to answer…

What tools do you need to use in your magical working, to make it magical?
What clothes (or lack thereof) do you need to wear in your magical working, to make it magical?

What scents do you need to have in order to make the magical working into an act of magic?

What lighting (or lack thereof) do you need to have in your magical working?

Now the answers to these questions may vary from magical working to magical working or they may not. It's your aesthetic, so remember that ultimately it boils down to what you feel is appropriate to your magical work and toward what will create the experience of magic. Yet there is also another factor to consider in this…

The role of your spirits in your Aesthetic of Magic

If you believe in spirits, then this section is relevant to you because your aesthetic of magic may not be entirely decided by you. A given spirit may have its own input about what constitutes a proper magical working. So keeping this in mind, here's a few additional questions:

What correspondences are associated with your spirit?

How does your spirit want those correspondences to show up in your magical work with it?

How does your spirit want its offerings made?

How does your spirit want its altar designed?

There are likely some other questions that could be considered, but these are a good place to start. You want to keep these questions in mind as you develop your relationship with your spirit and get the necessary input that can help you customize the experience you have with the spirit. Developing the Aesthetic of magic with a spirit is really about co-designing the working.

Why it can be useful to Question your Aesthetics of Magic

Now I want to explore why it's useful to question your aesthetics and how that can benefit your magical practice. While your aesthetics of magic is useful for helping you understand what makes a magic working magical, it's not a good idea to treat your aesthetics as set in stone. If anything, questioning your aesthetic filter can help you recognize how it might limit you magically, or what you could change about a magical working.

In the example, I used in the previous post, the person mentioned that sigils didn't look magical, which was why trying to do magic with them didn't work. One question I found myself asking was, "**What could this person change about the sigils to**

make them look magical (and therefore buy into them being a viable magical operation)?"

It's important to recognize that the Aesthetics isn't limited to the appearance. When I think of an aesthetics of magic, I'm thinking of what makes the experience magical, which can include (but is not limited to) visual appearance, but can also include the smells, sounds, feelings, taste, as well as movement and stillness (and whatever else you might think of that contributes to creating the experience). This distinction is important to note because if we're going to question our own aesthetics, we need to recognize what we are specifically focusing on. So how do we question our Aesthetics?

First you need to decide what is aesthetically part of your magical workings. I suggest looking at a number of magical workings you've done over a period of time to identify the aesthetic elements that consistently show up in those workings. This will tell you which aesthetic elements are considered necessary on your part in order to make a magical working happen.

For example if you find that you consistently use candles in your workings, then candles would be an essential aesthetic element of your magical practice.

Now take a look at what aesthetic elements don't show up in your ritual or workings. For instance, you might not do chanting, because you might think it's a distraction or that it doesn't sound magical (or whatever the reason is).

List the aesthetic elements that you consider essential in one column and in the other column put the elements that are non-essential.

Why are the aesthetic elements in the essential column necessary for your magical working?

This is the question to ask yourself. Beside each element write down your response. No answer is wrong. The point of this exercise is to understand what makes a given aesthetic element essential to your magical practice.

Why are the aesthetic elements in the non-essential column unnecessary for your magical working?

Just as with the previous question, write down why a given aesthetic element is unnecessary or not magical enough for you. Again there's no right or wrong answer. The point of this exercise is to help you understand why a given element isn't aesthetic enough for your workings.

Now it's time to try something new...

You know what the essential and non-essential aesthetic elements of magic are and why they are or aren't essential to your practice, but it can be a useful exercise to try something new with your magical practice. Try putting together a magical working where you don't use all the aesthetic elements you normally use, or where you mix in some aesthetics that you normally wouldn't use. Then record what the results are, but be willing to do this multiple times, to see if there are any differences.

Also if you're using an aesthetic element of magic that you normally wouldn't use, ask yourself what you could do to make it magical. Don't be afraid to make some changes. For instance, in the case where the sigils didn't appear magical, the person could try drawing the sigils differently or using colors or try a different sigil technique.

The benefit of experimenting with the aesthetic elements is that it gives you an opportunity to challenge what you consider to be essential. And even if you come away with realizing that what's essential is really what works to make a working magical, at least you've questioned and challenged your aesthetics and discovered for yourself why those elements are essential.

The benefit of working with aesthetic elements you don't consider essential is that it allows you to discover if you can make them essential to your practice and also provides you an opportunity to challenge your ideas about what is or isn't magical.

Lesson 9: Intention, Attention, and Magic

Intention is another vital principle of the magical process. For the purposes of this book, intention is volitional attention. In other words, it is focused attention that is dedicated toward a particular task or activity a person is doing. Typically when people discuss intention they talk about the motivations a person brings to an activity. Did they have good intentions? While motivation is important, by examining intention as a form of volitional attention, we can see that it is much more than just motivation. It is the actual application of motivation to action in a way that focuses the attention on fulfilling the motivation. Thus intention is focused attention directed toward accomplishing a specific goal, activity, or task. A magical working can be one such task.

It should also be noted that intention is an altered state of mind. The experience of intention can be likened to the psychological concept of flow, where a person enters a state of mind where they are highly focused on a specific task and lose track of time and everything else around them. A magical working can, when properly done, induce a state of flow. In fact people will describe an intense meditative state or magical working as one where their awareness of time was altered, while they were doing the ritual. The experience of flow also occurs when a person is intensely focused on any creative act. If you are writing, painting, or doing some other activity that involves hyper focused attention, you are entering into a state of flow. I've mapped intention to flow to demonstrate the importance of volitional attention and how it actually prompts this altered state of consciousness in magical work. If we don't bring intention to a magical working, what we are really losing is that key ability to focus on the execution of activities that will realize a specific outcome that we associate with the intention.

Not all forms of attention fit intention. Paying attention to TV or multi-tasking is a very different form of attention as compared to focused attention. When you are watching a TV show, your attention can be focused, but rarely is it focused on achieving an outcome. Instead it is a passive form of attention, with the person being more or less receptive to what s/he is watching. Multi-tasking, on the other hand, is a kind of attention that is focused on doing multiple activities at the same time. However, it is not focused attention, because you are having to split and shift your attention to different tasks and activities. It's also not as productive as people make it out to be. While a person may seem to be doing a lot, s/he doesn't get as much done precisely because s/he is having to shift back and forth between one activity or another. Multi-tasking is still a linear activity, precisely because you have to shift back and forth between activities.

When we think of intention or volitional attention, I think there are two key characteristics to consider. The first characteristic is the focus. You are focusing your attention on a specific activity, ritual, etc., for a period of time that is longer than just a second or a few minutes. You aren't multi-tasking, and any task you do, within this state of mind, is a result of your intention. In other words, your intention is directing and focusing the activities you do.

The second key characteristic is that intention is an active form of attention. You are doing activities that create and sustain that state of intention or flow. The activities are guided and defined by your intention in the sense that all of them are made relevant by how they feed and express your intention. The activities flow together to create a chain of action that builds your intention and focuses it on the outcome you are bringing into reality. Your intention is only released when you have done all of the activities necessary to express your intention while creating a path for the desired possibility to become reality.

Intention, as it relates to the magical process, can also be thought of as focusing the will of the magician. This principles of intention is present throughout the magical process. It fuels and directs the magical process. You've defined your result and now you need to set and focus your intention to start the process that turns the possibility into reality. Ideally, when setting your intention, you should have a good idea of any blockages or beliefs that might compromise your ability to fully realize that intention and the desired result. If you do discover such blockages, it's important to either assess whether you really need the result, or do internal work to undo the blockages. We'll cover how to do that internal work in later lessons. If, however, you find that all of you is completely in agreement with the result you want to manifest, then it's time to set intention and use it to guide your magical process.

How to Set Intention

Intention is volitional or directed attention. Setting intention involves picking an action that can be used to embody and express your intention in your magical process. That activity involves creating an altered state of consciousness that is representative of your focus. For magic to be effective, the magician needs to enter a state of mind where all possible distractions are ignored or removed, where what the magician is focused on is the process for manifesting the desired result s/he wants to obtain. In one sense, your intention is an obsession for the duration of the magical working, because it demands that your attention be completely focused on the process, ignoring all else. As such, an altered state of consciousness is ideal because any such state typically creates a hyper awareness of your process, while excluding anything else.

The altered state of consciousness needs to be one you can control. While some people like to employ entheogens (drugs) in their magical work, I don't recommend it as it ultimately puts you into a state where you aren't in control of yourself or your actions, which is the opposite of what we want when practicing magic. My own experiences with entheogens has shown me that any benefit is fairly limited, compared to a disciplined daily practice of magic, which can help you achieved altered states of focused attention readily.

There are two basic types of action a magician can take, both of which can produce an altered state of consciousness. The first type of action is inhibitory. It involves inhibiting sensory awareness in order to enter an altered state of consciousness. The second type of action is excitatory. It involves entering into an excited, hyper state of activity in order to enter into an altered state of mind. Both types of actions are equally effective for setting intention, though some people may find it easier to use one type of action over another. What's important is that the given action produces a state of intention which allows you to access the possibility you want to manifest into reality. We'll cover these types of actions in further depth in future lessons.

Some people think that setting intention is as simple as stating in a verbal or written format what your intention is, but that is new age thinking at its worst. An intention isn't set through a statement alone, but through directed and focused attention. If you can enter into an altered state of mind when writing or saying your statement of intent, *then* you have set your intention, but for the majority of people, it usually requires more effort and activity than just stating your intent. A person who can enter an altered state of mind by just making a statement is someone who has learned to discipline and focus the mind through years of daily practice. For the rest of us, however, it's important to use specific activities as part of the process of harnessing the attention effectively. This is why rituals, which can involve repetitive actions, are so effective. The repetition of the actions creates a rhythm that focuses the attention of the person on the magical process. This is also why tools and other such components can be useful. They help create the mood and focused intention that is necessary to successfully set intention. As such they become optional only when you don't need them anymore to reach that state of mind that allows you to set and direct your intention.

Not all magical activity is repetitious. Drawing a sigil isn't repetitious, but it can still be used to set the intention of the magician. What's really crucial about any activity you use for magical work is that it is an activity that focuses you completely and utterly on what you are trying to accomplish. Thus writing can be a magical activity (as Mr. Burroughs displayed time and again), and likewise painting can be a magical activity. Any act of creativity can be a magical act, which is why a paintbrush can be just as much a tool for magic, as a wand, and in some ways is more effective because you are using it to actively create something (which is an embodiment of magic if I ever saw one). The successful setting of intention is the creation of an altered state of mind where all that exists is the activity the magician is doing. Below are some questions to consider as you determine how you'll set intention.

What activities do I already do that create an altered state of mind for me?

What activity will best express my intention, and focus my attention?

What activity is challenging for me to do, but will also focus my attention?

I include that last question because sometimes the best way to set intention is to do something that you find challenging. The reason is simple. When you are doing something challenging it forces you to focus your full attention on doing it, in order to successfully learn it. Why not make all that effort count in your magical work? You can create a sigil to focus on as you do the activity, or chant a mantra, or do something else that allows you to draw on that effort and direct it to your magical objectives.

As I mentioned above, the act of creating something is an embodiment of magic. It's also an embodiment of intention, and this is why incorporating acts of creativity into your magical process can be one of the most effective ways of powering the process. A creative act is inherently magical because it is pulling a possibility into reality. Thus utilizing creative activities can be effective for enhancing your magical work.

However, we shouldn't rule destruction out either. The act of destruction can also be an embodiment of magic and intention. Destroying something you hate can take up quite a bit of focus. And destruction doesn't needed to be limited to an object of hatred. The destruction of something you made can be powerful. I've even found the act of quitting a job to be a powerful act of destruction. The choice to leave is a destruction of sorts that can be empowering, provided there is intention behind it.

The fact is that any activity that you put intention toward can be turned into a magical working, provided you can make a solid connection between the action and the magic you are working. Magic really can be as simple as that, but you have to understand how it all fits together for it to be consistently applicable, in my opinion. Intention, much like connection, is one of these essential principles that makes magic work.

Lesson 10: Inhibitory Actions and Magic

In the previous lesson I discussed inhibitory and exhibitory actions. These are types of actions that are essential to the success of your magical process because they produce an altered state of consciousness (or intention) that allows you to access and utilize magic to turn possibilities into reality. If you examine your magical workings, you'll note that an altered state of consciousness is a given for those workings. How you achieve that altered state is up to you. One of the reasons people do use ceremonial magic is because the ceremonies, tools, incense, oils, etc. are used to create a state of mind that enables access to magic, but as I've discussed in earlier lessons, all of that is by no means essential. What is essential is the achievement of an altered state of consciousness and your ability to focus your intention, while in that state, on the actual result you wish to accomplish. Whether that result is a practical change in your life circumstances or communion with a deity, it is key that you are able to put yourself into a mental space that allows for the shaping of reality.

You might wonder why everyday consciousness doesn't float the magical boat. It's a good question to ask. Let's consider everyday consciousness for a moment. All around you are distractions. Your cell phone, your social media, your television, your books, and other forms of media are distractions. Let's not forget other people, pets, and other distractions. Everyday consciousness isn't suited to magical work, because it's easily distracted by everything happening around it. And you've also got your internal dialogue, the monkey mind which is chattering away about that show you watched last night or how hot that guy or girl is who just walked by, or any number of other "important" details that grab its fancy. Everyday consciousness is constantly bombarded with information, distractions, emotions, etc. It's not ideal for magical work because it's very unfiltered. An altered state of consciousness, by contrast, is filtered in a very specific way. That filtration blocks out all the distractions so that the magician can focus his/her intention on accessing and directing the magic. I'll cover exhibitory actions in the next lesson, but for the moment let's focus on inhibitory actions.

Inhibitory actions involve inhibiting sensory information in order to force the magician's attention inward. The benefit of doing this is that it removes sensory distractions from the magician. At the same time it should be noted that there's no such thing as true sensory deprivation. The magician is always experiencing some kind of sensory information. Inhibitory actions nonetheless focus your consciousness on a very specific stimulus. Inhibitory activities typically take more discipline and dedicated time to learn than excitatory activities. The benefit however is that over time a person is able to enter into very deep altered states of mind and can apply the discipline to all magical activities (and for that matter to life in general). Because the focus is learning to quiet and focus the mind and senses, the magician ideally is using some type of inhibitory activity as part of their daily work, in order to enhance their skills and test their discipline. Below are some examples of inhibitory actions.

Meditation: The goal of meditation is to focus the attention of the person. While some will argue that successful meditation is being able to empty your mind, I'd argue that empty mind is just one form of meditation. Taoist Water Breathing Meditation doesn't focus on emptying the mind, but instead focuses on dissolving emotional, mental, and physical tension in the body in order to help the person circulate his/her internal energy or Chi. In fact, from my own studies, the majority of meditation techniques are less concerned with emptying the mind and more concerned with teaching a person how to harness his/her internal energy. The focus on the emptying your mind has more to do with Buddhist meditation than any other type of meditation system.

All the same, meditation does involve learning how to tune out or ignore sensory information and distractions occurring around you. Practicing Zazen or other meditation practices where you empty your mind can be good disciplinary tools for learning how to ignore sensory information around you, and for focusing your mind. A good meditator is someone who can meditate in diverse environments with different levels of noises and other such information without being disturbed by it. They will hear the noises, or see the people, but not acknowledge them, because they are able to ignore it as extraneous information. However doing that type of meditation takes a lot of practice. I suggest going to a public park where you can meditate without being disturbed, but will still be able to hear a variety of noises, as well as have access to a variety of other stimuli. When you meditate in such a setting focus on soaking in the sounds and other stimuli. Accept them as part of your environment and then detach yourself from them. They are part of you and part of your experience. Accepting them allows you to take them in and become one with your surroundings.

A good best practice for meditation is to focus on your breathing. When you inhale, breathe in with your diaphragm. There are different types of breathing, but with each type it's still important to breathe into your diaphragm. This will allow your stomach to expand and contract, while also building up your stomach hara, which is typically your center of gravity. This breathing practice also allows you to use the full capacity of your lungs and greatly aids in inducing an altered state of mind. Focusing on your breath can also teach you to be aware of your body and the way your internal energy flows. Because breath is a cycle it allows you to tap into the cycle of your internal energy and its circulation. Breath is the rhythm of your internal energy. If you've never meditated, or if you have but want a simple meditation technique to do, the following is one I've come up with, derived from other techniques I've learned:

Inhale and exhale through your nose. When you breathe in, mentally follow your breath to your diaphragm. When you breathe out mentally follow your breath out of your body. Do this the first 20 or so breaths, to establish an internal awareness of your body. Once you have that done, when you breathe in hold your breath for a second. Then exhale and hold it for a second before you inhale. Use the pauses to create a rhythm. That rhythm will draw your mind into a pattern of altered consciousness that you can use for magical work.

Another breathe exercise I like to use, which stimulates the internal energy or chi of the body is the macrocosmic fire breathing exercise. It's a Taoist breathing technique that involves the circulation of energy through your body, in order to raise that energy. You can use it to get a stimulating start to the day or use it to prep your energy for magical work. To start do the following: When you breath in, feel or visualize energy moving from your stomach to your crotch and then up your spine, to your head. When you exhale, feel or visualize that energy move from the crown of your head to your stomach, completing the cycle of movement. Once you've circulated your internal energy a few times, add the following. When you breathe in and you circulate the energy to your crotch and spine, feel or visualize it also going to your legs and arms. When you exhale and you bring the energy back to your stomach, feel or visualize the energy returning from your legs and arms. This can be a good exercise to stimulate your body with the internal energy you have available. One word of warning: If you feel a blockage or area of tension don't force the energy through the blockage. Let it move around it. Try both of these exercises out!

Sensory Deprivation: Sensory deprivation involves depriving yourself of one or more senses in order to focus your mind. There are multiple methods and tools of sensory deprivation. For example a sensory deprivation tank is a tool that a person can use to achieve an altered state of mind. The person is put into a tank of warm salted water, with no light. They will float in the water and lose sense of their body and in the process achieve an altered state. This can an excellent tool for doing internal work, or for doing astral projection or some other kind of work where you want to lose your awareness of your body, and be able to enter into a state of extreme altered awareness. But what if you don't have access to a sensory deprivation tank?

A bath with salted water can also be used as a sensory deprivation tank of sorts. It won't be quite the same but it works on the same principle. Turn out the lights and get the blinds shut and you can create something of an environment that's ideal for sensory deprivation. I've used this approach a few times, especially when doing work where I wanted to make contact with an entity, and have always found it to be a useful tool, because the senses are still deprived of a lot of stimulus. It's not the same as a sensory deprivation tank, but it's the next best thing when you don't have access to one.

Another method for sensory deprivation involves using some kind of bondage or restraint to limit your movement, or constrain it all together. Putting an eye cover over your eyes, ear plugs in your ears, or having your wrists and ankles bound to restrict them can induce a state of sensory deprivation that you can use to create an altered state of mind. When you find that you can't move or that one or more of your senses is somehow restrained it tends to sharpen the other senses, but it also sharpens the mind, which can then be directed. It's important to be careful with bondage. Make sure the skin has enough room to breathe and if your limbs start to get numb or if you feel pain beyond the acceptable discomfort, it's time to get out of the restraints. I recommend, if you don't have experience with bondage, going to a rope class or finding out if your local kink community is hosting classes on bondage. It may not be your kink, but you can learn a lot from people who use it as their kink.

There's also a type of therapy where an active limb is constrained in order to force a person to move a paralyzed limb. You can experiment with constraining just your legs or arms, to see if that puts you into altered state of mind. Or you could constrain one side of your body, but leave the other side free. There are definite ritual applications with all of this, if you choose to apply magic to such exercises. For example, you could choose to constrain your dominant writing hand, so as to use the other hand to write, and then use that exercise of writing (or drawing) for magical purposes.

Sensory deprivation is something you want to experiment with carefully. While it can definitely by used for magical workings, if you are choosing to use bondage or a sensory deprivation tank, you should have someone nearby who can monitor what is happening with you. And if you do feel physically uncomfortable, don't try to push past it. Acknowledge it and get yourself out of the restraints. Otherwise you could do physical and mental harm to yourself.

Dream Work: When you go to sleep you are shutting down your awareness of your body. Your dreams are a way for the mind to process information received during the day, but they are also much more than that. They can help you process past memories, allow you to fantasize about other worlds, or whatever else your imagination can conjure up. If you can enter into lucid dreams, you can use them to do internal work and for other magical activities. I have found *The Tibetan Yogas of Dream and Sleep* by Tenzin Wangyal Rinpoche to be helpful, partially because he provides specific exercises to do to help you induce a successful lucid dream state. There are also Western practices of dream work that can be useful. My wife has told me that in the Stregheria and Fire Temple traditions dream work is used to interact with spirit allies, in order to get information from them. There are also practices that focus on having the practitioner keep a dream journal, which can be useful for helping you remember dreams and analyze them later.

One exercise that I do, when I want to do dream work, is focusing on a particular person or topic of interest. I will usually associate a symbol with that person or topic. As I go to sleep I will visualize that image and use it to create a virtual world around me. I can use that virtual world to interact with the person or topic of interest. I've found that doing this allows me to enter into a lucid awareness of the dream. I also have good recall of the dream afterward. You can try this exercise as well. It can prove useful, especially when dealing with a problem situation. Your dream gives you a virtual environment to work in and resources you can devote to solving the problem. Some of my creative projects have come from using this approach.

Exercise

What inhibitory activities have you practiced? What role do these activities play in your magical work? How do you integrate them into your magical process? If you don't practice them, why not?

Lesson 11: Excitatory Actions and Magic

Excitatory actions are the second basic type of action that a magician can use to induce an altered state of mind. Excitatory actions involve hyperstimulating yourself through activity. A runner's high is an example of an excitatory action. The adrenalin caused by running helps to stimulate a euphoric state for the runner, which in turn can allow them to ignore more pain and tiredness. The benefit of doing excitatory actions is that they can help you achieve an altered state of mind in a relatively quick and easy fashion. However, it's also worth noting that some excitatory activities don't leave you with as much control. For some people that can be preferable, but it also has its own dangers, especially when doing magic, because it can open you up to unwanted influences.

Excitatory actions require less discipline on the part of the magician. Thus it might be tempting to cut corners and simply use excitatory actions to put yourself into an altered state of mind. However doing this cheats the magician, because as your body gets used to the excitatory action it takes more of that action to put you into that altered state of consciousness. In the short term you might achieve that state easily, but find it much harder to achieve down the line. Ideally the magician draws on both inhibitory and excitatory actions to put themselves into an altered state of consciousness. That way they are gifted in both approaches and can readily enter an altered state of consciousness using one type of action if the other type doesn't seem to be working. Additionally you may find that not all excitatory actions are equal, when it comes to achieving an altered state of consciousness. Some activities will interest you more, while others just may not be your cup of tea. Below are some examples of Excitatory Actions.

Running, Weight Lifting, & other Exercises: I mentioned the example of the runner's high earlier, but you can also experience such a high with other exercises. Exercising long enough will push the person into an altered state of mind that can be used to focus on a magical activity. I used to do a series of exercises that I would use for my daily practice, to help me exercise my body, while also using the exercise as a purging/purification from whatever issues I was dealing with at the time. It was definitely effective in both regards.

These kinds of exercises can be very helpful for tuning you into your body consciousness, as well as focusing your mind in general. The best thing to do is to focus your mind on feeling your body move and hold that awareness as you exercise. As you exercise, you can even use the burning of a calories as a fuel source for your magical work, in combination with the exercise itself. One practitioner I knew actually created a video game image of his ideal body, and when exercising visualized that body melding with his body. He eventually ended up looking like he wanted to using exercise, but also visualization to create this ideal appearance. There's a lot you can do with exercise and magic. I've used exercise as part of my daily practice, especially for purification purposes. As you exercise you sweat out the toxins in your body and the same can apply spiritually as well.

I've also found that exercising before I meditate can be very useful because the exercise has allowed me to clear my mind of distracting thoughts and leave it open and receptive to doing meditation. This has helped me achiever deeper states of meditation as a result. I've also used exercise to help me with memorizing. I will memorize words to a chant and then recite them to myself as I exercise. This simultaneously reinforces the memorization and embodies it in my body in motion, making what I've memorized into part of my identity.

Dancing: Dancing, especially combined with some kind of repetitive, rhythmic music can be used to induce an altered state of mind. I've also witnessed cases where a person would wear an animal skin and do a dance to the animal in order to create a trance state where she connected with the animal spirit. Dancing is particularly effective as a way to invoke the spirit, allowing it to possess your body and move it through dance. A person can just let themselves go in the movement and then invoke the spirit to allow it to take over.

However you can also use dance for other purposes. I like to use dance to embody a particular energy or space that I want to access. I've even used dance to explore different angles of spatial movement, such as moving diagonally. As it applies to magic dance can also be a good way to enter into a state of mind for charging a sigil or other magical working you are doing. Just as with exercise the real limit is your imagination.

Making Music/Singing: Making music or singing is another excitatory method for creating an altered state of mind. I've sometimes used singing in magical work to sing an enchantment. Likewise, I remember sitting in on jam sessions and afterwards hearing the musicians talk about how playing the music put them into an altered state of mind where they felt like they were merging with the universe. When singing I like to experiment with the range of vocalization that the throat offers. With the right pitch you can end up vibrating the words, which can be a very powerful magical tool, with invocations or with chanting. Additionally, some meditation techniques rely on mantras as part of the meditation. You will say a word or phrase again and again. When doing so you actually want to vibrate the word or phrase. That's what activates the altered state of consciousness.

Creating Art: Creating art can be another excitatory practice. The act of painting, sculpting, any other artistic activity, if done long enough, can create a state of flow. Beyond the state of flow, art is also useful as a magical tool because it allows you to portray different forces you are working with or specific realities you want to create. I use painting for a lot of my magical work, especially for evocations of entities. I'll paint the seal of the entity, as well as whatever other impressions I pick up. I then use that painting as a gateway to access that entity. The technique of automatic drawing is an example of an artistic excitatory action. The magician starts to draw and enters into a state of altered consciousness to do the entire drawing and use it for magical work.

Writing: Much like art, writing can also be used as an excitatory method. The cut-up technique that William S. Burroughs and Brion Gysin developed is a good example of an excitatory technique. You cut up magazines, newspapers and any other media with words and images and then reassemble them into your own message. You can also do stream of consciousness writing, where much as with automatic drawing, you start writing and you don't edit or direct the writing. You simply write it. Journaling can also be used for the same purpose, but you pick a specific theme or topic for the journal. In my own experiences with journal I've found a correlation between the topic I'm journaling about and experiences I'm having in my life at the time.

Entheogens: Entheogens are foreign substances used for the purpose of inducing an altered state of consciousness. Alcohol is an entheogen as are drugs, both legal and illegal. While these substances definitely work, it's worthwhile to be cautious in employing them, both in terms of avoiding addiction and also avoiding overreliance on them for achieving altered states of consciousness. If you use them regularly you'll need increasing amounts to achieve the same state, which obviously means you could be taking risks with your health. If you are going to use them, make sure you have someone on hand who can watch over you and keep notes. I do recommend keeping the usage to a minimum, as much for health reason as for discipline. If you rely on entheogens too much it can be hard to develop the discipline that the majority of magical practices require.

Video Games: I include video games, because of the sensory stimulation, and also because played long enough they can cause altered states of consciousness. I've used video games for sigil work and know of one case where a person used a game to help him coordinate his physical exercise. He created a character that represented him and used that character to model the changes he wanted to accomplish with his exercise. Video games can be addictive, so it's important to employ some caution in utilizing them for magical work. There are cases, particularly in South Korea, where people have killed themselves because they focused on playing games to the exclusion of anything else.

Also although games can lead you to an altered state of consciousness, they also imprint a lot of their own imagery on your consciousness. I've gone to sleep after playing a game for a few hours and had vivid dreams about the game. It's entertaining, but it does suck up valuable psychic resources and can even affect your imagination. I enjoy games, but I try to keep my imagination fed with a variety of other resources that aren't visual, but nonetheless allow me to explore it without relying too much on technology.

Yoga, Tai Chi, etc: Yoga, Tai Chi, and related activities use specific postures and motions to achieve an altered state of consciousness. Some movement is slow, some fast, all of it is used to create a hyper aware state of the movement. Moving meditation is an example of a hyper aware state. The focus is on doing the movements and using them to meditate in the process. This kind of movement is different from dancing, because the movement is far more controlled and focused. Moving meditation can be quite useful for both internal and external magical work. The movements can be thought of as aligning the magician with a particular goal or purpose, with each movement directing the magician toward that goal. The focus on movement is ideal for also focusing on the goal, and incorporating the purposeful movement into the achievement of the goal is useful because the movements condition the magician to pursue actions that will bring the goal about. Doing the moving meditation every day conditions the mind and body of the magician to achieve the goals s/he invests into the movements.

BDSM: BDSM involves using pain, either physical or emotional, to create an altered state of mind. It can also involve using sensuality and arousal for the same purposes. For some people a need to submit or dominate will also be part of what puts them into an altered state of mind. In BDSM, you can encounter cases where some use of sensory deprivation is involved, but it's usually done for the purposes of enhancing other senses. The end goal is to create an altered state, which along with the ritualistic aspects of BDSM, makes it ideal for magical workings. With that said, the majority of people involved in BDSM aren't magicians and typically don't approach it for spiritual purposes. You need to be picky in your choice of partner, so that you're working with someone who knows how to "switch" from the play aspect of kink to the ritual aspect you are using the kink for.

Sex: Sex has been used for magical purposes for a long time. Tantra and Taoism include sexual practices that can be used for magical purposes, and Western magical traditions also have sex magic practices. Whether a person is masturbating or is having sex with a partner or partners, sex can be used as an excitatory action. It does take some discipline and focused will to effectively use sex for magical purposes, and many people who think they are doing sex magic usually aren't, especially if they end up focusing on the pleasure to the exclusion of the specific purpose they are supposed to be focused on. While enjoying the pleasure of sex is always nice, in sex magic, pleasure isn't the objective. As such while you may feel pleasure, it's important to turn that feeling into the magical working itself, so that it fuels the working you are doing. I also recommend that you don't approach sex magic as a casual activity. In other words, your sex magic partner shouldn't be someone you pick up at a bar for some casual fun. It should be someone that you can connect with in a meaningful way. You are connecting your energy to the energy of that person and using the combination for your magical work. From past experience, I've found that casual partners don't work that well in a sex magic process, because they aren't committed to it in the way a more serious partner would be. This isn't to say that you need to be in a romantic partnership to do effective sex magic. What's important is that whoever you do sex magic with is someone you have a genuine connection to that isn't casual. It's someone you know that you can open up to on a variety of levels of your being and vice versa. What makes sex magic effective is the connection between you and your partner and how you apply your shared resources to the magical work you are doing.

Excitatory actions are useful for achieving an altered state of consciousness quickly. A person can get caught up in the feeling and sensations and use that to put them into the proper mental space to pursue magical work. But the magician shouldn't focus solely on using these types of activities. A good balance of inhibitory and excitatory actions is wise to cultivate. I've known people who tend to rely exclusively on excitatory actions for their magical work, and what I've found is they tend to be more stressed out and anxious and find it hard to do meaningful internal work. That said, excitatory actions are especially useful for doing magical work that is focused on the world around the magician. Since such actions already involve raising energy, the magician can easily direct that raised energy toward the specific problem or goal that they are using magic to achieve. As I mentioned above with moving meditation, the magician can imprint on themselves specific goals they wants to achieve by using excitatory actions. The actions will reinforce what the magician wants to achieve by fully conditioning the body and mind to achieve those goals.

Homework

What excitatory activities have you practiced? What role do these activities play in your magical work? How do you integrate them into your magical process? Pick one or two activities you haven't used and use them in your next ritual to achieve an altered state of mind.

Lesson 12: Internal Work

Internal work is an integral activity of the process of magic, but it's also an activity that is sometimes ignored in magical work, to the detriment of the magician. This isn't surprising, however when you consider that the emphasis in modern occultism is on achieving measurable, practical results, and also on reactively using magic to solve problems, as opposed to applying a more proactive approach to magic. It doesn't help that Western magic typically doesn't provide much in the way of meditation techniques that are necessary for doing internal work. I, and others, have had to look into Eastern spiritual practices such as Buddhism, Tantra, Bon, and Taoist practices to discover meditation techniques that can be used to work with and refine the internal reality of the magician.

Some will argue that Kabbalah and Alchemy provide such approaches, but Kabbalah, while providing a mystical tradition, doesn't provide a focus on doing internal work so much as providing a map to work with as well as entities to draw on for that work. Likewise alchemy can provide some avenues for internal work, both through the psychological interpretation and the lab work version of it, but the psychological approach doesn't provide the same experience as lab work does and the problem with lab work is that you have to be able to afford all the equipment for lab work as well as finding someone who can and will teach it to you (At this time I know of one person who teaches lab alchemy in the Pacific Northwest).

There's also the eight circuit model that Timothy Leary and Robert Anton Wilson developed, which is useful as a diagnostic tool for internal issues. Recently Antero Alli evolved the eight circuit model to include physiological work, which has enhanced how it can be used for internal work. Pathworking which is a form of visualization can also be used for internal work as Nick Farrell demonstrates in *Magical Imagination*. I've developed a system of internal work based off working with elemental spirits. For the most part, however, these various techniques either rely on psychology or on working with external forces to do internal work. Eastern practices focus on the person doing internal work, without necessarily relying on external forces or psychological perspectives. None of them are better than the others, and all of them can be combined to develop an integrated approach to internal work.

Internal work is working with your values, beliefs, dysfunctional issues, and overall outlook on life. However internal work also applies to the mastering of your life energy, or chi. Thus it's important not to mistake it as a wholly psychological approach to magic. If anything internal work applies an energetic and physiological approach to what is typically thought of as psychological issues. That dysfunctional issue of depression or anxiety isn't perceived as a purely mental issue. Instead internal work recognizes that there is a physiological and energetic component to it as well. Granted, psychologists and neuroscientists recognize that there is a physiological side to a psychological issue, but the approach to dealing with such an issue typically relies on drugs to manage the issue, whereas an internal work approach focuses on working with and through the issue. For example, in Taoist water breathing meditation, the magician focuses on dissolving internal blocks. These internal blocks are energetic, emotional, and physiological. When the magician does the breathing practice s/he uses the circulation of the chi to discover where the blockage is manifesting itself as stress in the body. Then s/he starts to dissolve it, using the energy to gradually and persistently pull apart or melt the blockage. When this occurs emotions and memories may come up and need to be worked through, in order to help with the dissolution of the blockage. The end result is a freeing of internal energy as well as a release of the emotional issue.

If you are taking medicine to manage a psychological issue, I urge you to continue to take it. But you can also use internal work to help you manage the issue as well. You may find that if you work with it long enough that you may not need to rely on medicine, but if you choose to pursue that route, do so carefully and keep good records of the work you are doing so you can determine, with your doctor, if there is a legitimate reason to scale down or get off of medication.

I'm going to present you with a couple of meditation practices that you can start doing now. I recommend integrating at least one of them into your daily work, so that you can benefit from them. However, I also want to point that when you do this work, you are doing it to change your internal reality. As such you may find that you end up dealing with unresolved feelings and memories you'd blocked away. This can be good, in terms of allowing you to resolve those feelings and memories, provided you are prepared to do so. I've been doing internal work since 2005, and I've found that it has significantly improved my life by allowing me to resolve and work through issues I hadn't been facing directly but which showed up in my life through the various problems I continued to encounter. And that is actually the most essential reason for doing internal work. Even if you choose not to do it, you'll find that your life circumstances will reflect those unresolved issues. The more chaotic your life is, the more internal issues you likely have that need to be resolved. Working through those issues via internal work can bring a lot of peace to your life, both in terms of the situations you encounter and your overall sense of well-being. I also recommend supplementing your internal work with therapy. A good therapist can help you by giving you a sounding board to discuss the issues that you are encountering, as well as providing his/her own perspective on those issues.

The first meditation practice is Taoist Water Breathing Meditation. The water breathing refers to the type of breathing you are doing and is also associated with how you move your internal energy as well as how you deal with internal blockages. With this breathing you want to touch the tip of your tongue to the roof of your mouth, to connect the internal pathways of your energy. In Taoist water breathing, when you inhale, you draw the chi from your belly up to your crown, and when you exhale, you release that energy and allow it to flow down your body.

This differs from the fire breathing exercise, in terms of the direction of energy, but also how you work with it.

With water breathing, when you release the energy from the crown of your head, you don't direct it to a specific place. Instead you allow it to flow down your body, and you use it to identify places where you feel physical and energetic tension in your body. You don't want to force the energy through the tension, but rather allow it to flow around the tension, gradually dissolving it. Think of it as water flowing around and gradually dissolving ice, or like picking apart a knot. It's going to be a gradual easing of the tension which in turn releases the energy behind the tension. Don't be surprised, when you do this breathing, if you feel emotions or memories come up. The key is to not repress them or block them out! Allow yourself to feel the emotions and memories. It may be a bit painful, but you will find that if you do so that it releases the tension and allows you to move on from those emotions and memories. I recommend doing this breathing every day. I've used it to work through a variety of issues, and have found that not only have I been able to move past those issues, but it's also energized me. Releasing the tension has freed up a lot of internal energy that was held in the blockage. The release of that energy has been beneficial for my health and sense of well-being. A book I'd recommend, if you want to learn about this technique is Relaxing into your Being: Breathing, Chi, and Releasing the Ego by B. K. Frantzis.

The second technique involves personifying your internal tension into a "demon" that you can interact with. This technique is especially helpful for dealing with internal messages that you tell yourself such as "I'm a bad person". You visualize the tension, stress, or emotion as a demon. You can visualize it having scales, horns, or whatever else helps you visualize the stress or emotion as a separate entity. Once you have personified it you can enter into a dialogue with it. First you ask it what it wants. Usually it'll tell you the self-destructive message it represents. Then ask it what it needs. Typically what it needs is some kind of emotion, such as love or acceptance. Visualize yourself giving as much of the emotion to it as it can handle. When it is satisfied it might change its appearance. Then you can ask if it is now your ally and how it can help you.

This technique can be helpful for changing internal dialogues and interacting with your internal issues. You aren't creating an entity so much as creating a way to dialogue with what you want to change. I've found it helpful for learning why I'm sabotaging myself and for making changes to that behavior. If you want to learn more, I recommend reading Feeding Your Demons by Tsultrim Allione, which covers the technique in more depth.

There are a variety of internal work techniques that you can learn. I recommend learning some type of meditation that you can do on a daily basis, to use for the purpose of working through any issues you have as well as working through what your beliefs and values are and how they apply to the world. Doing dedicated internal work will change you, in terms of how you perceive yourself, the world, and even in the need for magical work. I've found that my approach to magic has significantly changed from being reactive to being much more proactive and focused.

One technique I develop for internal work is the elemental balancing ritual. In this ritual, you dedicate a year of your life to working with a particular element that represents an area of your life you need to work with. For example, if you feel ungrounded in life and don't have a solid grasp you might work with the element of Earth. The benefit would be that you would use the element of earth to learn how to become more grounded and how to work with practical areas of your life such as finances. You don't have to work with the classic elements of Earth, Air, Fire, Water, and Spirit either. For example, I've worked with the elements of Time, Space, Emptiness, and Identity. I consider all of these to be elemental forces because they are forces that effect our lives on a regular basis. Time is a force we talk about and interact with each day. It is primal and it is something that moves us. It's similar to the classic elements, as are the others I mentioned. Other people who've used this technique have worked with movement as an element. It really comes down to what you consider to be an element.

To do this working you identify what element you feel you need to work with in your life. When I first developed this ritual, I chose water because I wasn't in touch with my emotions and I wanted to learn how to work with them and I associated water with emotion. Think about an area of your life that you want to work with and ask yourself what element you'd associate with it. Once you pick the element you'll want to do a pathworking to connect with the elemental energy.

In the pathworking you want to put yourself into a meditative trance. One technique I do involves gradually causing your body to relax so you can enter into a receptive state of mind. You count from 1 to 100, but you break into increments of 10. Use the following script to help you:

As I count from 1 to 10, I will feel a tingling, relaxing energy start at the tip of my toes and go up to my ankle relaxing all the muscles in my feet and ankles.

As I count from 11 to 20, I will feel the tingling relaxing energy move from my ankles to my knees, relaxing the muscles in my calves, even as my feet become more and more relaxed.

As I count from 21 to 30, I will feel the tingling relaxing energy move from my knees to my hips, relaxing all the muscles in my thighs, even as my lower legs and feet become more and more relaxed.

As I count from 31 to 40, I will feel the tingling relaxing energy start at the tip of my fingers and move up to my wrists, relaxing all the muscles in my hands, even as the same energy relaxes my legs and feet.

As I count from 41 to 50, I will feel the tingling relaxing energy move from my wrists to my elbows, relaxing all the muscles in my forearms, even as my hands, legs, and feet become more and more relaxed.

As I count from 51 to 60, I will feel the tingling relaxing energy move from my elbows to my shoulders, relaxing all the muscles in my upper arms, even as my forearms, hands, legs, and feet become more and more relaxed.

As I count from 61 to 70, I will feel the tingling relaxing energy move from my hips to my shoulders, relaxing all the muscles in my stomach, chest, and back, even as my hands, arms, legs, and feet become more and more relaxed.

As I count from 71 to 80, I will feel the tingling relaxing energy move from shoulders to my neck, relaxing all the muscles in my neck, even as the rest of my body becomes more and more relaxed.

As I count from 81 to 90, I will feel the tingling, relaxing energy move from neck up to the top of my head, relaxing all the muscles in my scalp and face, even as the rest of my body becomes more and more relaxed.

As I count from 91 to 100, I will become more and more relaxed. When I count 100, I will see a door, and the door will open to the elemental realm I wish to work with. I will ask for an elemental spirit to appear before me in a shape and form I can recognize.

Once the elemental spirit appears, ask it for a symbol and also to tell you about the element and how it could help you with your life. You might wish to use this pathworking a few times before doing the ritual. I suggest recording yourself saying the script out loud if you want to listen to it, but not say it, while trying to do the pathworking.

When you do the ritual to dedicate yourself to an element for a year, you'll use the symbol to invoke the element into your life for that year. Don't be surprised if the elemental spirit shows up over the course of the year to work with you and provide advice. The ritual itself can be done in any particular way you like. I've painted the symbol on my forehead and then come up with a poetic invocation that I've chanted aloud to invoke the elemental energy into my life. I've also created a water color painting of the elemental symbol and then performed sex magic via masturbation to anoint the painting with my fluid, which in turn activates the elemental energy. Whatever ritual you come up with will work, provided you are able to make a viable connection to the elemental spirit you want to invoke.

These yearlong workings can be intense. You'll find yourself going through a lot of changes, both internally and in your interactions with others, but those changes are beneficial in terms of helping refine who you are so that you are more balanced in your life.

Lesson 13: Spiritual allies and the magical process

This lesson takes our focus on the process of magic, in a different direction, specifically as it applies to working with spiritual allies. While it's important to master your internal reality, it's also important to know what allies and resources to draw on to help you with that goal, as well as handling more mundane situations.

Depending on the situation, you may find it useful to work with a spirit ally or entity. I define spirits as objective entities that can be worked with or with whom a working relationship has been established. I don't think of them as inherently superior or inferior to myself. They are just different kinds of beings that exist on a different plane of existence. I do think of them as objective beings, as opposed to arguing that they are psychological constructs. With that said, as we'll see, there are elements of subjective meaning that can be applied to any and all entities that humans can work with. The reasons you might want to work with a spirit is as follows:

It has particular influence over a specific element of life. For example the Goetic demon Bune is attributed to having influence over wealth and death. In general spirits have specific realms of influence they have power over. I'll discuss why they have that power in further detail below.

It has the requisite objective distance from the situation to help provide a favorable resolution to it. This is especially useful when you don't have that objective distance.

It can teach you specific information or provide answers to questions you have about a specific situation.

You wish to exchange some of your essence for its essence in order to have more of a connection with the power it can access.

All of these are valid reasons for working with spiritual allies, and there are undoubtedly other reasons as well. In consideration to the magical process, it's important to note that how you approach an entity is at least as important as what it is that you'll ask it to do. What I mean by approach is not a question of method or technique, but rather a question of etiquette.

There are generally three approaches people take to working with entities. One approach involves summoning the entity and commanding it to do something, while threatening it with harm from other entities if it doesn't do what you ask. The magician who takes this approach generally spends a lot of time putting together protective spells beforehand, because if s/he loses control of the entity, it will undoubtedly decide to try and harm the magician. I've never tried this approach and don't advocate for it. It's an approach based on fear and antagonism, and even in the cases where it is successful, the magician always has to look out afterwards, because the entity will remember how it was treated.

The second approach is to summon the entity and make a bargain with it. I'm not talking about selling your soul or any other nonsense, but rather having a conversation where you discover what the entity wants in return for it performing specific activities for you. Using the example of Bune again, I did a working where I wanted him to help me get more business opportunities. In return for providing those opportunities, I agreed to write about him and how he helped me out. He wanted more attention and awareness directed his way. Remember to always fulfill your end of the bargain. This approach is based on respect and a desire to mutually benefit each other. All of my workings with entities have been very successful and there's been no spirit ally drama in my life afterwards.

The third approach is worship. By worshipping the entity, the person provides attention and belief, while also placing the entity into a higher hierarchical position compared to him/herself. The person might pray or ask the entity for aid, and sometimes the entity will provide aid, but this is solely at its whim and decision. This approach is based on subservience to the entity, though there may also be feelings of love associated with the worship. Again, this isn't an approach I've used, though others have. It provides some degree of success, but the success is based entirely on the entity's choice to intervene.

Types of Entities

There are multiple types of entities. Below is a basic descriptor of some of the types.

Deities: otherwise known as gods. These are entities that are worshipped. They usually have specific realms of influence that they have power over and they also either have a lot of attention being directed toward them, or in the past have had a lot of attention directed toward them. Some of these entities are ancient and some are relatively new. All of them seem to rely on and desire attention, belief, and worship as a way of fueling their power and influence on this plane of existence. My own work with deities has involved taking a different approach. I respect them, but I won't worship them.

Daimons: sometimes known as demons. Daimons are spirits of wisdom. The use of the word demon arises from Christianity's corruption of the word, and is also reflective of how Christians view such spirits. For all intents and purposes these are spirits that provide information on very specific topics. I haven't found any of them to be overly malevolent or interested in my soul. What they seem to value is being treated with respect. When I've worked with demons, they have usually wanted me to write about them or otherwise show information about them, in order to increase people's awareness of them. Just as with deities, I take an approach of respect and I will bargain with them. I don't worship them.

Angels: In Christian mythology, angels are perceived as opposites of demons. You'll also see a lot of imagery of cute cherubs with harps, but I don't think that's an accurate perception of angels. If we trace the history of angels further back, we find they are not cute or innocent cherubs, but rather spirits of power and authority that usually act as interfaces to other energies. For example, in traditional hermetic magic, the angels Uriel, Raphael, Michael, and Gabriel are guardians of the elemental energies. In order to work with the elemental spirits, you needed to first work with the respective angel guardian. What's important to understand is that both angels and demons represent specific concepts or attributes.

Faeries: Spirits of the Earth and land, and also of the Fey. When I think of faeries, I think of both the Daoine Sidhe, and also the wee folk. In some traditions they are associated with elemental spirits, likely due to the association they have with the Earth and the land. It's important to treat the faerie with respect and pay close attention to the wording of your requests. They don't seem to need attention or belief...their interest in communicating with us seems to be more out of curiosity.

Elementals: Spirits that are connected to specific elemental energies of Earth, Air, Water, and Fire, and responsible for keeping the elements balanced. They aren't necessarily interested in contacting us, but they are open to being contacted. I've done a lot of work with elementals and have found they are interested in exchanging their essence for my essence. The result has been a closer connections to the elements. In my own experimentation, I've explored the possibility of their being elemental spirits for sound, love, emptiness, and other concepts that I'd argue are relevant to the human condition. I don't know that the entities I've worked with are necessarily the same kind of elemental as the basic four elements, but working with them has proven helpful in making changes in my life. My inspiration for doing this kind of elemental work was based off the recognition that human attributes are assigned to the basic elemental energies. Working with those energies can also help you work with those attributes, and by extension the elemental work I've done with non-traditional elements has been applied in a similar fashion.

Created Entities: Entities created for a specific purpose or objective. Also known as servitors and egregores. Egregores are created entities that have gained enough influence and recognition that multiple people are working with them. Servitors are entities that one or two people are working with. These entities need to be fueled and the usual fuel is belief or attention of some kind.

Some Considerations about Entities

I mentioned earlier that spirit allies or entities are objective beings. I also think they are symbiotic beings, to one degree or another. They may or may not be symbiotically linked to humans, but I think they are symbiotically linked to this world, and would even go so far as to argue that they are an essential part of what causes life to exist on this world. With that said, I also think it's important to recognize how much cultural beliefs about entities have shaped our own relationship with entities.

In the majority of cultures that exist, there has typically been a relationship where humans worship deities, pray to them for solutions, and in turn make offerings to show their respect for the entities. Deities are entities that have been given a lot of attention and belief, enough so to supply them with more power than they might otherwise have. Nonetheless, if we were to take away all that attention and belief, the power would dry up fairly quick and the god might not exist, or if it did exist, it would be in a significantly different state. As blasphemous as that may sound, if we look at the dynamics of a relationship between a deity and a person, what we find is a need for attention and belief from the person in order to fuel the existence and power of the god. If we look at various mythologies we see this theme occur again and again. Gods demand worship in return for sparingly providing miracles, which in turn are used as proof of their power and reasons for why they should continue to be worshipped.

But obviously not all entities are the same. Daimons aren't gods, and neither are Angels, Faeries, or elementals. Nonetheless, an interesting theme occurs with some of these types of entities, a theme of bargaining, where something is exchanged in order to obtain something from the entity. And what's always stressed is how important it is to examine the letter of the bargain and then make sure you do your end. Even when the theme of bargaining or worship doesn't show up, there is still a theme of respect and the need to establish a respectful relationship. I'd argue that respect is the most important ingredient in doing a magical working with an entity. I always try to establish a relationship of mutual respect with any entities I work with.

In summation, whatever relationships you create and cultivate with entities, make sure that you understand what the give and take of those relationships are. Breaking your word with a magical entity is never something to do lightly. It always has consequences and those consequences can create a lot of havoc in your life, or the lives of people around you.

Where do entities fit into the magical process?

We have a symbiotic relationship with entities or spiritual allies and as such we can work with them quite successfully to bring desired results into our lives. We shouldn't rule out working with them either, because there will be situations where it's clearly advantageous to work with them. Entities fit into your magical process in situations where you are too close to the problem, or in situations where you need information or opportunities sent your way and you don't have the times or resources to obtain what's needed without some spiritual help on the side. I advocate taking the middle road in working with entities, namely bargaining for what you want, in return for providing something they want, and doing all of it with respect. Even with created entities, you will need to think about what you can offer that will provide them the necessary energy to accomplish what you want them to achieve (See Creating Magical Entities for more information).

As with any magical technique, it's wise to not overly rely upon entities. Knowing when and how to work with them is more important than indiscriminately evoking them whenever an issue arises. They want to know we can solve our problems, without always having to go to them. For example, I work with entities that provide me awareness of opportunities I might otherwise miss out on, but I don't have those entities actually manifest the opportunity. I leave that up to myself, so that I can continue to grow, both as a magician and a person. That, ideally, is how you should approach entity work in your magical process.

Exercise

What role have entities occupied in your magical practice? If you've never worked with them, why not? If you have worked with them, in what capacity have you worked with them and how has that shaped your magical practice?

Read Creating Magical Entities. Create a magical entity, using the entity creation sheet, to solve a specific problem in your life or to aid you in resolving that problem.

Lesson 14: Techniques and the Process of Magic

The process of magic is realized through the application of specific techniques that are used to direct magical power toward achieving specific goals and results. There are eight essential techniques that a magician utilizes when doing magic. Although we might come up with a variety of derivatives of these techniques, from my own observations it seems that all derivations ultimately boil down to these eight techniques. What's truly important is knowing when to use a given technique. Not all are equal for each situation. Below is an overview of each technique.

Invocation: This is an act that involves drawing an entity or person's consciousness into your own for either partial or full possession. The benefit of doing this can be to obtain information, achieve union with an entity, or as part of an offering ritual to the entity. I've experimented with the process of invoking one's self into an entity or person, because I've found that invocation is a two-way street. Invoking yourself into someone else can used to help that person work through a trauma, though it can also be used for less ethical purposes.

Evocation: This is an act which involves evoking the entity (or person) into the environment around you. Evocation can also be used to evoke emotional forces or behaviors so that you can work with them in an external environment. Evocation is typically used when you want to manifest a specific possibility and need help from an entity to accomplish the task.

Divination: If you want to obtain information, divination is technique that can be used. It typically involves using Tarot, runes, ogam, or some other kind of symbol set that is randomly shuffled or mixed before he person draws and then places the cards, runes, ogam, etc. into specific patterns. The cards, runes, ogam are read in order to obtain the information that is desired. There are also other techniques of divination, that rely on entheogens or other forms of hyper stimulation in order to create visions the person can then interpret. Divination can also be used to examine past and present influences or variables to determine how they influence the current situation you're in.

Enchantment: An enchantment is an act of magic that is directly done by the magician to bring a specific possibility into reality. The magician directly applies magical force in order to make the possibility into a reality. The magician achieves this using a variety of tools, such as sigils, tarot cards, ceremonial tools, etc. The choice of tool is dependent on the magician's system or methodology of practice.

Banishing: Banishing is used by the magician to ground and center him/herself, while cleaning the space of any unwanted forces or energy. Banishing can also be used as part of daily practices to help focus the mind and will of the magician.

Astral projection: Astral projection is where the magician projects his/her spirit or mind into the astral planes. The magician will do this in order to do a magical working on those planes or to access resources that wouldn't be found here. My personal take on the astral planes is that it's partially derived from our imagination and is where we can directly interact with imaginary time in order to find possibilities that we'd like to bring back with us to reality. Astral projection can also be used to connect with past and/or future magical personalities, geographic locations, and/or entities.

Meditation: Meditation is a technique that can be used to ground your mind, focus your will, empty yourself, or otherwise be used for internal work. There are a variety of types of meditation, and the different types do serve different purposes. A meditation to do internal work with the consciousness of your body will differ from a pathworking you do to work with a psychological issue, but different types of meditation can be used collaboratively for doing internal work. We've covered meditation in lesson 11, so we won't cover it in any further detail.

Attunement: Attunement is a technique where you attune yourself to a particular energy or sensation. It can be similar to invocation, but it's not used with entities, so much as it is used to connect with the land around you, or with the ocean, or with any other raw, primeval force. Attunement is a way to integrate yourself with magical forces that you can draw on and use for other magical work.

Lesson 15: Invocation 1

Traditional invocation is a technique magicians use to connect with entities. Invocation involves allowing the entity to access your consciousness and take partial or full control of your body. Invocation is done for a variety of reasons.

Information: Invoking an entity can give a person access to the entity's knowledge, though usually the entity will want something in return. Since invocation is the easiest way to pass information along, what the entity usually wants is the opportunity to enjoy some time in the person's body, having experiences it might not normally have. The magician will share consciousness with the entity, allowing it a taste of his/her experiences. The entity will provide the information in return, so that the magician has access to it when needed. This type of invocation could be considered a form of divination, though usually it's for very specific information the magician wants.

Possession: Sometimes an entity will be invoked in order to give it possession of the invoker's body. For example, in voudon, the invoker will allow the loa to fully take over his/her body. This type of possession isn't limited to just voudoun, but you are less likely to encounter in other traditions. With this type of invocation, it is very important that the magician has other people on hand, both to keep his/her body safe, and to keep an eye on what the entity is doing, while also recording any information it offers. When the person is possessed s/he will move differently than normal, may talk in a different language, and otherwise will act like the entity. The entity will use the possession to express itself, not just in language, but in movement, and in whatever other ways it can, in order to convey its message to other people.

Healing: An entity can be invoked to help in a healing ritual. The magician will invoke such an entity when s/he wants to heal someone and wants to draw on resources the entity can offer to help with the healing. The benefit of invoking an entity is that it can help guide you as you're doing your healing work on the person. You can also invoke an entity when you want to ask it to heal you. This can be useful, because the entity is drawing on its own energy, as opposed to drawing on the impaired resources of the body.

Worship: In a religious context, an entity is invoked as a way to worship it. The person who invokes it may or may not allow full possession. S/he will channel it, so that the worshippers can interact with the entity. The ritual that's performed to invoke the entity is part of the worship process.

Non-Traditional Invocation

I mentioned traditional invocation, which implies that there is non-traditional invocation, and in fact there is. I developed non-traditional techniques, when I realized that invocation is a two way street. In other words, if I can invoke an entity into me, it stands to reason that I can also invoke myself into the entity. Pathworking can actually be used for that purpose. Invocation works on a principle of identification. In order to successfully invoke an entity, the magician needs to identify with the entity, and through that identification provide a pathway that it can use to access the body, mind, and spirit of the magician. This same pathway and identification can also be used to invoke yourself into the entity. It's a matter of being able to understand it enough to access its consciousness. I've found this type of invocation most useful for obtaining information from the entity, but it can also be useful in a situation where you want to do an exchange of essence with the entity. By being able to access the entity in its native environment, you can get a better handle on the essence it provides you, in return for what you give to it.

You can also invoke yourself into a person. Since invocation is based on connection, if you can connect with the person, you can invoke yourself into him/her. I've invoked myself into people to help them unblock or heal themselves. I've also used this practice as a way of aligning with other people when we do long distance rituals. This kind of invocation should only be done with the permission of the person you are invoking yourself into. It's important to remember that you will be getting access to that person's emotions, memories, etc., but that person will also be getting access to you and could just as easily invoke him/herself into you. Let's take a more in-depth look at invocation.

In the anime series *Neon Genesis Evangelion*, Evangelions (aka Evas) are mecha (giant robots), replicated from the angel Adam Kadmon (in Kabbalah known as the quintessential man): a combination of flesh and machine. The pilots have to enter an entry plug, termed the throne of the soul, before they can actually get into the Evangelions. The pilots are actually souls and the entry plug serves as the housing for the soul within the Evangelion. For the Evangelion to operate, the pilot and the Eva must synchronize. This synchronization is achieved partially through technology; specifically the pilot's neural signals become the central nervous system for the Evangelion. But sometimes it's also achieved by the pilot's will power, so the soul of the pilot is essential for the Eva to work. The synchronization of Eva and pilot creates a god that not only fights the angels, but can also serve as a medium of evolution for humanity. And all of this is achieved through the pilot being invoked into the Eva, as opposed to a more traditional approach toward invocation.

Invocation is traditionally treated within magical workings as a process where you call a god/goddess or other entity into you. When you invoke an entity, you invite it into yourself. Depending on how strict you are with the invocation, the entity can even use your body as a medium, or can simply be in the ritual to share its consciousness with yours. An invocation allows it to "ride" in your body, though generally not to the point of being ridden (possessed) in the Voodoo paradigm or similar cases of trance possession. Another definition of invocation is William G. Gray's definition, where he argues that invocation involves calling inwardly. This means internalizing the invocatory call to mesh the person's internal sense of self with the force s/he is invoking. In other words, an invocation is successful when you can align your internal reality with the reality of the entity you seek to invoke. When that alignment occurs, the connection is made and the invocation successfully occurs. This definition of invocation is one that closely resonates with how I approach invocation, namely using it as a way of connecting or strengthening existing connections between myself and others, be they entities, godforms, or people. I also find that Bardon's energy impregnation technique helps with this connection. With each inhalation of breath, vital energy is absorbed and then exhaled and returned. A magician can isolate a particular energetic frequency and infuse that frequency into their own energy, in order to invoke the entity.

The ultimate idea of an invocation is to build up a resonance of energy between yourself and what is invoked so that you not only channel the force you're calling, but share energy with that force. In fact, invocation is a synthesis or synchronization of the person and the entity being invoked, so that the energy created by the connection is a melding of the caller and the called. Invocation not only affects the invoker, but is linked to the other people who are doing the work with that person. In other words, those people are also drawn into that invocation and to a lesser degree invoke the entity into themselves in order to relate to it and the work it's doing through the invoker. It's not just a single person doing the invocation, but ideally the group of people.

A truly effective invocation creates a synthesis of energy between all the participants and the entities called. The spoken word is treated pure vibration and energy, which penetrates through time and space to connect invoker with the invoked.

What's really incredible, though, is that if a person hits the right vibration (vibrato) they can actually synchronize their mind to the theta wave state of the brain. This altered state of mind is a liminal zone between waking and sleeping, and as such is devoid of the censorship the subconscious mind would exercise over the conscious mind. This access is perfect for invocation workings, because it's an optimal opening of the mind of the magician to another force and vice versa. With a vibrato tone of the voice the magician can consciously put themselves into that state of mind, making both invocation and any space/time activity easier to manifest. The penetration of time and space occurs when the entity invoked is in two realities at the same time, its own reality and this reality, through the medium of the invoker. The harmony of this occurrence is established through the sounds and vibrations which create a sympathetic resonance so that the entity can exist in both places.

Invocation can be used with more than just the traditional method. In the example above the invocation that is achieved is manifested through a merging of the Eva and the pilot, but the merging occurs as a result of the pilot being invoked *into* the Eva as opposed to invoking the Eva into themselves. So what ends up happening is that the invoker "rides" the invoked godform, a reversal of the usual process. Or in the case of Eva, they meets the godform halfway so that the invocation is mutual. The actual invocation won't happen until the conjoining of the pilot's soul with the Eva's essence occurs. It's possible within magic to do such invocations and more.

The invoker does need to resonate or have a form of sympathetic connection to make this kind of magic work. You can invoke yourself into godforms, entities, or for that matter, people. Pathworking is a form of invocation, but instead of the invocant calling the godform to them, they go to the godform, essentially invoking themselves into the godform as a way of knowing it better. The pathworking is simply a reversal of energy flow, or, if you will, linkage. When a person does invocation they are creating a link for the entity to travel to them or for them to travel to the entity. The key aspect of invocation is the link itself and the value you place in it, which acts as a road or a bridge. The value is the effort you put into maintaining the connection. Any relationship you have needs effort to sustain itself. When you stop calling a friend, the value you place in that relationship is diminished, because the effort is lessened. The same applies to the entities you work with. How much do you value the connection you make with something else? The value shows in the relationship you establish with others. If you don't make the effort to keep the connection going, then the entity or person will likely not make that much effort either. Value shows even with the connection you establish with yourself, in terms of how you take care of your needs and present yourself to other people. If you have low self-esteem, other people will know it and treat you accordingly. Value sets the tone of the resonance you share with another person or an entity.

These interactions you have with people every day are a form of invocation. You invoke the reality of the people you interact with. You even have a version of that person inside of you (i.e. you have a perception of who that person is, how s/he acts) and so every time you see or hear from that person, you invoke the reality you know. And by extension the people you know also have a version of you within themselves. You even have your own version of yourself within you, the observer observing the person who acts. All of these versions contain an aspect of the truth about you. The invocation of you is achieved every day through the rapport and connection you build between yourself and a person, and even between yourself and the version of yourself within that person.

We use invocation in our lives to help us navigate through the various situations we encounter in life. For instance when I taught my students while in grad school, I invoked a persona of myself that was an effective teacher. Likewise the various other functions I'm engaged in inform the invocation of the various roles I adopt to fit the expectations of the people. For instance, when I do a workshop on magic, I'm expected to be at least somewhat knowledgeable in the subject I'm discussing. As such when I'm doing my workshop I'm bringing forth the various magical experiences and knowledge that I've had so that I can provide all of that in the workshop.

It may seem that I'm blowing invocation out of proportion, but it's important to understand that a magical concept/tool such as invocation is used every day in ways we don't expect, and that if we are aware of invocation in this way, we can begin to appreciate how it can be used outside of the formal settings that it's traditionally used in. We can make invocation into a very practical and flexible form of magic. But we have to apply it beyond how it's normally considered.

Part of this application is the invocation of the self into the godform, entity, or other person. By learning to work with the connection we have manifested we can come to a greater understanding of the forces we work with and how the interaction affects us and them. The benefit is that you also get a sense of the god's perspective, how they perceive and understand you. The limitation is that you are visiting where the entity exists. In other words, you are visiting that god or spirit's actual environment or plane of existence. This principle of invocation is the same as pathworking, except that instead of creating the environment that you'll be visiting, the entity has created it. I have not noted any dangers in doing this kind of invocation, but I have always done it with the permission of the entity I'm invoking into.

A technique for invocation that may be useful in maintaining the connection with the entity, whether you invoke yourself into it or vice versa, is to come up with a costume that represents the godform. This works particularly well with pop culture personae, though with enough creativity and research you can likely come up with a costume that represents a godform from any period of history. When you put on the costume, which represents your connection to the godform, invoke yourself into the godform. What'll you be doing is using the costume as the medium for the godform. The costume will act as a shell or housing for the entity. If you take the costume off, the invocation ends.

I mentioned earlier that sometimes I invoke myself into a person. This kind of invocation happens due to the connection you have to the person and specifically to the version of you that exists within that person's conceptual mind. You don't need a strong information connection to do this kind of work successfully, though it can help. Nor do you need a strong emotional connection, but again it helps. What you need is a solid understanding of how energy works, and specifically how first contact already enables you to do this kind of invocation regardless of how well you know a person or are emotionally invested in said person. In the initial contact with anything you establish an energetic connection, and it's that connection by which invocation occurs.

I've done this form of invocation with a number of people in varying situations. For this lesson, I will draw on four case studies. One person lives in the U.K. and she and I are doing magical workings with the Dehara system of magic. Because I live in the U.S. it is naturally hard to meet in person. Sometimes when we have synchronized rituals, we have invoked each other. We've both noted the strength of presence we feel in doing this technique as well as how intimate such invocation becomes. In one sense, you're sharing your soul with the person you invoke yourself into. The phrasing I've used when invoking myself into this person is Astale (name of person or "I invoke myself into the person" or both). The actual physical distance has not been a significant detractor in the strength of the invocations and we've only met once in person. Numerous online conversations have helped to create a link between us, as well as creating the Dehara system of magic. But for all intents and purposes, though we know each other well, what has really created the link between us isn't the physical proximity, but rather the desire to use invocation as a medium of connection that enables us to flesh this magical system out further.

I also used this technique of invoking myself into another person who was one of my lovers. Because she and I lived some distance from each other and I saw her rarely, I used this technique to close the gap, as well as gain a better appreciation and knowing of her. However my invocation with her was different from that of the person in the U.K. I wasn't actually involved in ritual when I did this invocation. Instead, I used meditative trance, taking one hundred breaths to synchronize myself and then saying: "I invoke myself into (name of the person)." These journeys into her psyche had been intriguing, giving me glimpses of magical workings she'd done, entities she worked with, and even past lives she may have lived. In one journey I even found myself in a place where I looked into file cabinets and saw various ritual tools in the cabinets. In these journeys there were walls or partitions which represented the mental boundaries that she had in place. I wisely respected those boundaries. When I told her of the journeys she verified the details I gave her. Since we broke up, I don't do the invocations into her anymore, beyond one last journey I did, which I used as a way of closing the connection and saying farewell. I think that this kind of invocation goes past the surface of the soul and into the true essence of the person you work with.

In the third case study, I decided to work with a fellow magician. However, this person lives in the Ukraine. My initial contact with her was through the medium of LiveJournal and subsequent contact with her occurred online through IMs. I know very little about this person and have virtually no emotional investment in her. Nonetheless, the first night we chatted online, I decided to try and invoke myself into her and have her invoke herself into me. The connection was instantaneous for both parties. As a test we decided to describe each other to the other person. I had never seen a picture of her, but was able to describe not only what she was wearing, but the color and length of her hair, as well as her eye color. Likewise she was able to describe me. Although we don't chat often, we've continued to use this technique as an effective way of teaching each other magic. What's enabled the success of this invocation has been the focus on feeling the energetic signature of the person. The communication through IMs served as an effective focus on her energy as well as a pathway to connect with her. The variables of knowing and having emotional feelings don't seem to be significant in this case, in terms of the strength of connection. What matters is that you resonate on some level with the person. Resonance isn't a factor of emotion or information, but of connection. Can you connect with the person, even a little? If you can, then invocation can occur.

The fourth case study involved connecting with a friend of a friend. I don't know this person and in fact mainly got involved in healing him because one of my best friends was very distressed about this, and I wanted to help him by helping his friend. In the healing ritual I did, I used Reiki as well as working with Verrier and Verrine, two demons of healing from the demonolatry tradition. These demons, along with the Reiki, guided me to the person in question, allowing me to connect with him and start the healing. I actually felt like I was in his body, made contact with him, and was even given advice by him for a couple of my own situations. Subsequent healings directed toward him have followed the flow of energy first established by the demons and Reiki. I will admit I used external help (i.e. the two demons) to make this connection occur, but again, the fact that external help can enable this suggests that the process of invoking oneself into another person is not determined by emotional investment or how well you know a person. Rather it's determined by how well you can synch yourself to that person's energy, emotionally or otherwise, using whatever available methods you have at hand.

I've also used invocation into another person as a way of doing energy work, meshing my energy with the other person's energy. In Taoist sex magic techniques, the emphasis is on circulating the energy through the bodies of both partners. While this cycling is occurring you merge your partner's energetic pattern with your own. You'll probably feel warmer or cooler, or a tingling sensation, which means the energy work is occurring. Both people can adjust the energy of the other person as well as their own to harmonize the synchronization. This refinement increases the output of the energy for both people, because while they are drawing on each other, they are also temporarily increasing the amount of energy available to each. When sex magic is practiced this way, the people aren't exhausted, unless the energy is directed away from them. The way you mesh the energy with the other person involves coordinating your breathing with that person's breathing so that when you breathe in (drawing your energy to you) that person breathes out, pushing their energy toward you and vice versa. The use of breath to coordinate the energy work, also can help coordinate the sexual actions, whether penetrative or oral. The energy work also serves to invoke the other person into you, because you are cycling that person's energy through you, as well as your own.

Recently two friends of mine used this invocation technique to go on a vision quest. They were both writers who sabotaged their own respective successes at business and writing, by making bad decisions that on reflection they knew not to make. The goal was to identify this sabotage chip in each other and then help the other person get rid of it. This demanded complete honesty from both people. They had to examine all the situations in their lives where they'd sabotaged themselves and missed out on an opportunity. Both of them picked a physical object to represent the sabotage chip. They put into or onto that object sigils that represented each moment they'd sabotaged an opportunity in their lives. Then they invoked themselves into each other and found the sabotage chip within and destroyed it. After the meditation the two people took the physical objects and destroyed them. This kind of invocation can be used as a general healing technique, because it allows both people to help each other cooperatively, without co-dependently relying on the other person.

If a person has a health problem, the invoker can try some healing work by finding the problem and describing it to the other person; this information can then be taken to a doctor to verify if it's correct. Additionally, the invoker can work some healing magic that will help the ill person resist the health problem or heal it all together. The invoker does this by adding their own energy to the sick person's energy, or they can choose to take the sickness from the sick person when they leaves. The latter approach is similar to sin-eating and other shamanic techniques, which involve taking the illness out of the patient's body and putting it into the practitioner's body. The problem with the latter technique is that there's a good chance you'll have to fight the sickness off, especially if you don't ground or banish the illness from yourself soon after the ritual. On the other hand, it can also be a useful method for assimilating the memory and energy of the sickness into your body, so that if you ever need to call that experience forth you can simply invoke that energy and then use the feeling of sickness in whatever way is appropriate. I've used to it as a shield to keep people away from me—nobody wants to be around someone who has the air of illness around them whether there are actual germs about or not!

Lesson 16: Invocation 2

In the previous lesson we discussed some of the means that invocation could be employed in your magical work when it comes to working with entities and other people, but in this lesson we're going to change the focus to where invocation applies to identity work.

Identity is central to the practice of magic. In choosing an identity, a person provides themselves a foundation. The identity may change as a result of the magic, but it gives magic something to act on and from. It is the basis by which a person forms an agreement with the universe as to their place within it. Magic is used to not merely change circumstances, but also the actual identity of the person. For example, when a person focuses on spirituality, above anything else, and has a belief that the body is not part of spirituality, the identity that they take on is not merely that of a spiritually focused person, but likely also someone in poor physical health, because that is the identity they have manifested with the universe. It anchors a person's connection to other places, people, events, etc.; and yet, as we'll see, identity is fluid. What we cling to with identity is not so much who we think we are, but rather the behaviors and patterns that are reactions to situations and experiences. Identity is related to media, in the sense that different forms of media can be used to change the identity of a given person.

Often our identities are dictated to us by the various circumstances we're in, without us fully realizing it. When a person goes into work they are expected to modify their behavior to conform to the workplace, by being cheerful and punctual, and suppressing signs of resentment. Likewise parents are expected to be patient, firm, and nurturing. These personality traits are created by expectations, which tell us the ideal reaction to have to a given situation. Even a person's ego, which is usually thought of as identity and individuality, is a construct formed by cultural and social pressures which, dependent on the culture, can make the conception of ego and identity radically different from one culture to another. Nonetheless, no matter the culture, the ego serves a common goal in upholding the status quo of the social consensus. The social consensus is comprised of custom, convention, and the range and structure of language. To protect a social reality, the identity of ego is important, for it constrains the person to fit into social norms. The ego isn't really identity, so much as a façade of identity, full of expected reactions and triggers that serve to define and control a person, while also judging everything around it to determine if it's suitable to that person.

When an entity is invoked into you, your behavior is temporarily altered. When we consciously examine these reactions and triggers, we can change the underlying behavior, which in turn dissolves the ego boundaries. At that point our identities have changed, no longer wrapped up in previous behavior patterns, or societal norms. We can consciously choose the identity we wish to manifest into reality. Invocation plays into this work, because it invades many of the ego boundaries with the presence of another being, that when called on, can impart its own sense of self, which can radically alter the ego's understanding of what is and isn't acceptable. Invocation plays an integral role in the formation of identity, as ego is left behind.

As a practical demonstration of what I'm writing about, consider this example from my own life. One meme I've had to work with is a fear of success. When I was a child I was taught that even if I was successful promises wouldn't be followed through on, or if they were, shortly thereafter what had been given as a reward was taken away from me. This early negative behavior led me to believe that even if I was successful the success would just be taken away. Later imprinting led me to also believe that any success I gained would only be gained through lots of struggle and obstacles. As a result I had a deep fear of success ingrained into me until I decided to consciously transform those behavior patterns into healthier behaviors.

One of my methods for changing this behavior involved using invocation via video games, specifically invoking yourself into a character and drawing from it specific character traits you want to embody in your own life. By adopting the identity of the video game character temporarily, I leave myself open to whatever I charge that identity with. Playing video games, for me, involves a state of no-mind, of receptiveness. I found myself identifying with characters and I began paying close attention to what traits I identified with the most that I thought could help me change my fear of success. Then when I played the game, I invoked myself into the character, drew on the specific traits I wanted to incorporate into my identity and brought them back into me when I finished playing the game. I treated myself as an empty vessel and filled myself with the specific behaviors that would change my attitude and beliefs about success. You could do the same with a deity or other more traditional entities.

Uploading the self is a variation of my technique of invoking yourself into another person or a godform. Invocation shapes the identity through assumption of another presence, and can be used consciously to work with and shape your identity in particular directions. In *The Matrix,* for people to enter the computer world, they had to upload themselves into the computer world. At that point, they could download information and skills into their virtual persona. They could also die there and the bodies would die if the persona did, because so much of their personalities were invested in the archetype. Your personality isn't nearly as nebulous as it may seem. It's this fact that's essential to really understanding the full potential of invocation or uploading the self into cyberspace. Your conscious sense of identity is limited, and that limitation often causes you to miss out on the potential that an aspect of your identity can offer you. An example of a personality aspect that many people take for granted is the body. We all have one, but we don't necessarily pay as much attention to it and how it shapes our perceptions of the world.

The body you inhabit is a reality in and of itself, but it's also a reality you've constructed through your perceptions of it. In other words, your perception of your body creates a residual self-image that you use when visualizing yourself. This self-image may not be accurate to the actual reality of your body. However, a person's perception can shape reality, and this includes the body consciousness. In fact, how you feel about your body, or how you imagine it appears, will affect how you present yourself to other people. If you think you are beautiful then you will act beautiful. The body consciousness has its own input and personality aspect that interfaces with the ego. The survival instincts that most people have are an example of the body consciousness taking an active role. We don't think about it when the body consciousness takes over, but it's a part of our personality wired to protect the mortal existence of the body. Unfortunately many people aren't consciously aware of the body consciousness.

The residual self-image is an identity point, a way of anchoring your personality to something familiar to you, such as your body. The self-image is the ego of the person, and it filters out whatever doesn't fit it. At the same time this self-image, and indeed all aspects of your personality, rely on the physical body to establish a sense of reality. One of the functions that the five senses of sight, hearing, touch, smell, and taste have is the ability to help the person construct a sense of reality and self.

We rely on our senses to provide us perceptions, but they also create our ability to sense, and make sense of, reality. Sight, as another example, allows a person to construct an object, its depth or dimensions, its surface appearance and texture, and even the movement, or lack thereof, of the object. At the same time, our senses also help in the construction of identity a person has. They are the medium through which we experience the self and the personalities of other people. In fact, I think that the reason people personify objects is because of the need to find identity in what is around them, as a way of constructing and grounding the self.

What this means is that some people will have a self-image that may only partially use the body as an anchor for the reality of the personality. Other residual self-images may be used that don't draw on the body you live in, but may draw on archetypes you identify with. These archetypes could include an animal, ancient god forms, or even modern pop icons. The body is only one facet of the self-image, but regardless of what your self-image is based on, your body will influence how you conceive of yourself when you invoke yourself into another person, upload yourself into cyberspace, play video games, or any other interactive activity. The body plays an integral role in allowing you to identify as something, because of the kinesthetic sense. This sense is your awareness of your body, and yet it also seems to extend outward toward whatever you connect with. In the process of playing a game, our senses extend to the character we play, to some degree, enough that a person can feel like s/he becomes that character. When I play games, I feel connected to the character to the point that I can feel the movement the character is engaging in. It's a subtle sensation, but identification with the character is imparted by it. Consequently the kinesthetic sense is not just responsible for our awareness of our body, but also anything else we happen to identify with and can be helpful for invoking yourself into another person.

Uploading yourself into a character, or into the internet itself, raises questions as to the nature of the mind. Can the personality be constrained to a body? If we can accept that the act of invocation is a reality that allows contact between the minds of humans and other entities, then it stands to reason that invocation as a form of uploading can be used to access virtual worlds and inhabit virtual bodies. While I don't advocate escapism into virtual reality, I nonetheless think it's time we challenge what the internet and these games are used for. Do we continue to focus only on entertainment or accessing information, or do we do more? Do we put these virtual realities to use beyond entertainment? Do we take control of these virtual realities that have a very real effect on us, or do we let them control us? Uploading yourself into the internet or game is the first step of many we can take to shape the virtual reality as we shape mundane reality. At the same time reality and identity are interwoven, and so alteration of reality is also a change of identity. The choice really, to evolve, to grow, to experiment, is your own. Where will you take yourself? That question can only begin to be answered when we start experimenting further with uploading the self into a virtual reality and question consequently what really defines reality, our notions of it, and how we want to shape all of it to accomplish our goals.

Acting and Identity

As I mentioned earlier, Acting is another way that identity can be shaped. The phrase "getting into character" is an excellent denotation of invocation and personality aspecting. In fact, in some cases, acting out a character can take over the life of an actor, as in the case of Tom Baker, one of the Dr. Who's that (according to at least one fan of the show) stayed in character even when he wasn't on the set. He knew that people wanted to interview Dr. Who, not the actor, so he let that identity completely take over the core personality of Tom Baker every second of the day.

Even when acting doesn't go that far, it still has useful methods for helping people come into character. Michael Ironside, the voice actor for video game character Sam Fisher from *Splinter Cell,* explains that when he tries to get into character he focuses on "six to eight levels of emotion. If it's a violent character I base the emotions on fear." (*Splinter Cell* interview 2003). He further divides the spectrum of emotions into two principles, love and fear (*Splinter Cell* interview 2003). Emotions are important in aspecting and invocation for two reasons. First, e-motions are energy in motion, which means they are a source of energy directed by the person toward a particular goal. Additionally, emotions can represent different personality aspects that people have, but haven't necessarily communicated much with. Most people, for instance, are probably uncomfortable with the emotions of hate or anger. How many times have you walked up to someone and said you hated that person? Probably not often, if at all. As an experiment I once walked up to someone I did hate and told her I hated her. It was a liberating experience. It felt good to honestly tell her how I felt. And having expressed that emotion, it no longer bothered me to feel it. I had acknowledged it and in doing so taken the power from it, reclaiming it for myself. But many times people will avoid uncomfortable emotions. Personality aspecting and invocation can help people come to terms with those emotions by bringing out the parts of the self that specialize in them.

Both in video games and in movies, there's a need to identify key traits of a character. In *Final Fantasy X*, the character designers were given key words to describe different characters. All of these key characteristics defined this character and how the voice actor would give him a way of expressing himself. The word cheerful describes the ideal emotional makeup of the character, while athlete provides an idea of the body type. Each attribute adds to the personality, which in turn brings life to the character. Even though Tidus is in a video game, people still get caught up in the story he tells. In the mind of the player, for as long as the game is on, Tidus is a real person.

Kratos from *God of War* is another example of a character with specific attributes and behaviors. He has life in the mind of the players. The game developers intentionally did this because they wanted a character that could let the players release their darkest violent fantasies.

In addition to creating a believable character, the developers of the game also made certain that the players knew they were playing a game set in ancient Greece. The various mythological monsters, while interpreted by the designers, were still recognizable as part of the Greek mythos. The best aspect of this game is that it drew on Greek mythology, but it also got inspiration from the series of 20th century movies such as *Jason and the Argonauts*, which depicted modern retellings of Greek mythology. In a sense, the Greek mythology was remade into pop culture, with Kratos as the central character. For Hellenic purists Kratos and other aspects of the game wouldn't fit what they considered accurate of Greek beliefs and magic (of course, neither would *Clash of the Titans*!). Nonetheless, the game is a good example of how older beliefs can be taken and re-presented in contemporary contexts. Kratos is an archetype that can be worked with, though carefully, given that he was created to channel the violence of people playing the game.

Real life actors also have to make the characters they portray realistic enough to have a presence in the mind of the viewer. When viewers see Tom Cruise in a movie, ideally they won't think of him as Tom Cruise. Instead they'll think of him as the character he's portraying. This applies to all actors. If the viewers don't believe the actor is the character, then they hasn't done their job. They need to play the role of the character to the point that s/he becomes that character. In effect s/he invokes the persona of the character so that it supersedes their own reality. A good way to find out how actors do this is to watch the documentaries and commentaries on the movies and TV shows the actor is in. If you're like me and prefer owning (or at least renting) DVDs, the special features will usually include interviews that may include the actor explaining how they get into role and becomes their character.

One thing I noticed in my research was that for the duration of the filming many actors tended to put their own lives and personalities on the back burner and assume the identity of the character, even when offstage. The actors will also spend hours a day just acquiring skills that the character would have. Tom Cruise regularly spends hours learning the particular skills his characters have so that those skills come naturally to him. Likewise the actor studies the mannerisms and behaviors the character might, usually by living or interacting with people who have similar behaviors. For instance, Leonardo DiCaprio spent time with OCD patients so that he could understand Howard Hughes better, in order to play him in the movie *Aviator*. Zhang Ziyi spent two months with a blind person to learn how she moved so that she could play such a character in *The House of Flying Daggers*. In each case, the actor spent a lot of time observing and/or acquiring skills, and in some cases changing their bodies, to become the character. Another fact I learned in my research was that actors would develop the character's history. They would get pictures of where s/he was from and what s/he did before the actual movie. The idea is to know enough about the character so that even though the viewer doesn't know those things, the actor can still use them to enhance the character's personality. They will provide some contextual clues about the past of the character, but even if the viewer never knows the entirety of the character's history, the actor will still be able make the viewer feel like the character has more of a life than just two hours (or less) on a silver screen.

Another aspect that is played with in media is color. The character of Vincent in *Collateral* is dressed in a gray suit, and speckled white and black hair and a beard, denoting his status as a liminal and amoral character. In the movie *Hero*, color is used even more ambitiously. Depending on who is telling the story, the costumes of the characters are different colors. The only character whose costume color is the same throughout the story is the unnamed character (*Jet Li*). The color of his clothing is always black, and represents both his mission, and the other characters' perceptions of him. The color changes for the other characters denote the changing of the seasons, but also the emotions of the characters as perceived by whoever is telling the story.

Color is used in a similar way in comics to signify the archetypal force the character represents; if we see the colors blue, red, and yellow we'll likely think of Superman. This is useful for us, because we can use those colors and costume to connect with the character in question. In fact, actors use colors and costumes to help themselves get into character. The colors and costume represents a gateway into the character.

I don't think magicians doing invocation need to go to quite the extreme that successful actors do when getting into character. However, there's something to be said for studying what actors do and learning from it. For an actor to be successful they must be disciplined in their training and in being able to subsume their own personality to that of the character. Additionally, the actor deals with emotional states and uses them to invoke a character. These skills are useful to the magician who must be comfortable with their own emotional states and be able to use them to create a sympathetic connection with a person or entity in order to do successful invocation.

The next time you watch a show or a movie and you really like the acting, do some research about the actor. Find out how they approached and became that character. Then incorporate their approaches into your own magical work. Chances are you'll find it to be a useful exercise that'll help you achieve better results with invocation. Rule no possibility out when it comes to getting inspiration for how you do magic.

Invocation of specific characteristics

Another approach to invocation involves invoking specific characteristics or traits of an entity. You don't necessarily want to work with the entire entity, which might have issues you'd prefer to avoid transferring on to yourself. However you want to work with specific attributes the entity has, or if you like you want to work with a specific face of the entity. It can be useful to invoke just that attribute or aspect of the entity, to draw on the characteristics that you need for a given situation. And the reason you want to do this is to infuse your identity with specific attributes that the entity embodies. For this kind of technique, it is useful to study some acting techniques, because an actor needs to be able to selectively embody an emotion or concept sometimes. It can be useful for you to learn such skills and apply them to your invocations, as a way of inviting in those specific attributes you want to learn, as well as for conditioning your behavior and identity.

Think of a character or an entity. Think about what traits you want to invoke. How does the character act when exhibiting these traits? What clothing, movements, etc. does this character have? What can you do to mimic said character, especially the particular traits you want to draw on? Use that action to create an anchor that links you to that attribute. When you need to draw on it, do the action or wear the piece of clothing that helps you invoke it into your actions and behaviors. Instead of assuming the identity of the character through invocation, create a blended identity, where you draw on the specific behaviors you want to have access to, changing who you not someone new, but not assuming the identity of another being altogether. I call this approach aspecting.

I was first introduced to aspecting as a magical act through another magician's experiment with creating four aspects of her identity that drew on different parts of her personality. She based these aspects off the Leary-Wilson model of the eight circuits of the brain, as described by Wilson in *Prometheus Rising*. Her four aspects drew on Wilson's observations on the four personalities of transactional analysis. She combined this experimental psychology with animal totemism. Two of her aspects were wolves, one representing hostile weakness and the other friendly weakness. The other two were a cougar representing hostile strength, and a cat that represented friendly strength. She used these aspects to explore facets of her identity that she knew existed, but hadn't felt fully comfortable exploring. This allowed her to experiment with different personality traits and get a sense of how those traits fit into her life. She based the animals off of totemic entities that could guide her in creating believable personality aspects that she could use in getting to know herself better. By distancing the behavior from the sense of self, the magician can comfortably deal with it and make peace with it, before integrating it back into themselves.

Likewise, in hindsight, I realized that my interaction with different pop culture characters allowed me to explore facets of my personality. I would use the aspects of them to safely explore those personality traits until I felt I could integrate my understanding of those traits into my identity on a conscious level. When I'm playing a game I'll find myself identifying with some of the characters I really like. Later on I'll think of those characters when I'm facing a difficult situation and end up invoking them to draw on the characteristic traits that I feel will help me face the situation. By invoking Guan Yu (the Chinese god of detectives and just wars, but also a character in a video game and actual historical personage) for instance, I could draw on his ability to be a commanding presence. This allowed me to enhance my own presence, so that I stood out more and had control of the situation.

I use pop culture entities as masks for my aspects. The character provides a familiar face and enough distance from my own personality that I can observe a particular behavior in the character and find similar points of reference in myself. At that point, I use the character to either enhance the behavior pattern or I can banish the behavior into the character. I then banish the character, removing its energy and sustainment of the behavior from me.

Even though the pop culture character is invoked and acts as an aspect there is always a distance between yourself and the entity. Invocation, even when it involves possession, can also involve keeping some level of awareness of your own consciousness. In the case of the actor Tom Baker, though the persona of Dr. Who had taken over, his core personality was still aware and conscious to some degree.

The most important feature of aspecting is that it allows you to shape your identity through conscious work via invocation of different entities and working with them as aspects of yourself, as you simultaneously call on both the entity *and the corresponding part of yourself*. The entities serve as references for a personality aspect you create, or you interact with them directly. In a psychological model, you make a conscious choice to understand and work with the personality traits of yourself that exist on a subconscious level and bring them to a conscious awareness so that you can determine how they fit into your life. The best way to do aspecting is to determine first what personality traits you want to work with. Then pick an archetype that resonates with those personality traits. Find out as much information as possible about the specific manifestation of the archetype you work with as well as similar entities (i.e. ones who'd fit the same archetype. As an example Loki and Coyote would both fit the trickster archetype, though in different ways). You may find that one of those entities resonates with you better than your initial choice.

Once you have all the information in hand, it's time to actually work with the entity. Neopagans routinely dress as the deities they invoke during ritual. In fan culture, costumes are used all the time to help the fan become the character they want to be. Therefore you may find costumery to be useful. You might also want other artifacts about the entity on hand, such as pictures, comic books or books on mythology. Also any incense, music, etc. that is associated with the entity is a nice touch. All of these artifacts can help you integrate the identity of the entity into your own identity.

When you treat the entity as a separate being, you'll need to carefully consider how you want this entity to work with you as an aspect. The first invocation is the establishment of the connection you share with the entity and your opportunity to explain what it is you want to do and how you want to do it. You'll want to be respectful, but also firm. You'll work with the entity directly while invoking it, drawing on its personality traits to influence your personality and drawing forth the corresponding parts of yourself. You'll need to identify traits within your personality that correlate with the entity. For instance, if it's a trickster entity, you would want to look at your sense of humor and how it will be impacted by working with the entity. If it's a warrior entity, you might want to examine your current martial skills, or how you handle emotions such as anger, as these can be impacted by the entity. Because you don't want it to have an undue amount of influence over your personality or behavior, you'll have to make sure that the connection can be stopped at any time. I usually choose to link the invocation to a specific object, so that when I want to aspect I can just wear the object and channel the entity into me, while at the same time retaining enough control to actually appreciate the effects of working with the personality traits I want to discover. When I want to stop working with the entity, I take the object off and the invocation ends.

Once I've worked with the entity long enough to get a sense of how its personality traits mesh with my own, I can create an amalgamation of myself and that entity which becomes my personality aspect. Basically I create a splinter personality which embodies specific behavioral traits, which I can use to help me deal with situations where it's needed, but still provide me some distance from the personality trait until I feel ready to integrate it into me fully. I no longer need to call on an external entity to accomplish this goal, because I'm using the personality aspect I've created. For example, instead of calling on Guan Yu to help me enhance my presence, I would call on a personality aspect inside me that took traits from Guan Yu and melded them into my behavior traits which also embody a commanding presence. By being able to call on and visualize a personality trait that embodied myself, but also had some of the skills that I'd previously perceived I didn't have, I could gradually integrate those skills into my psyche, while still providing myself enough internal space to get fully comfortable with those personality traits.

Identity is a fairly flexible concept. It gets shaped and altered all the time. Who you were one moment ago is different from who you are now. But you can consciously shape your identity and it behooves us all to do so, instead of letting our subconscious impulses rule over us. Invocation, in all of its many forms, is one of the ways we change identity. Most people think of invocation as doing that particular function, but they ignore the reality that invocation necessarily involves allowing your personality to be compromised with that of another. The questions are what can we learn from that experience and how will we use it to change our identity to get the most out of it?

Invocation's Role in the Magical Process

We've covered invocation fairly extensively in this lesson and the last one. It's a useful technique for doing internal work in terms of grafting specific behaviors onto your identity, and also for getting information or channeling a specific force. Rarely is the technique of invocation the only technique you'll use in your magical process. For example, I tend to combine invocation, with evocation, which we'll discuss in the next lesson.

Exercise

I want you to do an invocation of an entity or of a behavior you want to add to your identity. How does working with the entity change your sense of self and personality? Are the changes desirable or not?

Lesson 17: Evocation 1

In the lesson on spiritual allies, we covered some of the information about evocation, and if you've read Creating Magical Entities you now know how to create a magical entity, which is a form of evocation, in and of itself. This lesson and the next one explores evocation in terms of working with existing entities.

Traditional evocation is a technique magicians use to work with entities. It differs from invocation in that the magician is summoning the entity into the environment around him/her. Evocation is typically used to summon an entity so that it can perform a specific task that the magician requests of it. Some forms of evocation involve summoning an entity and then compelling it to aid you by invoking other entities that are opposite of it. For example, if I were to summon a goetic demon using traditional evocation, I would compel it to do a desired task by calling on angels to threaten it into obedience. This essentially amounts to threatening the entity into doing the task for you. I recommend against it, and would suggest collaboratively working with the entity, and honoring whatever activities need to be done to show your good will.

It's more accurate to call traditional evocation "medieval evocation", because the majority of grimoires and the overall approach come from the medieval time period and may actually be derived from more ancient practices. Traditional evocation usually involves calling upon daimons and spirits in order to acquire information, order them to do tasks, or work with the realm of influence the spirits happened to represent. Most, if not all, of the entities dealt with had specific spheres of influence and tasks (or if you will specific forms of media) they could help magicians with. As an example, the goetic daimon Ronove is skilled in rhetoric and linguistic skills. A magician would evoke Ronove in order to acquire these skills or improve upon them.

To summon a spirit, the magician needed to know the sigil or seal of the spirit and would also need to know the appearance of the entity. The magician used the characteristics and form of the spirit in conjunction with the sigil/seal to summon it. Knowing all of this information was also important in order to determine if the spirit called forth was really the spirit you wanted. In the medieval grimoires, the spirits were considered to be dangerous entities that would try to deceive and trick the magician in order to get free of the evocation.

Although knowing the features and characteristics is important, the sigil/seal is even more important. Franz Bardon lists three types of seals the magician can use for evocation: traditional, universal, and personal. The traditional seals come from the entities themselves and the magician must be able to project himself in their realm in order to get this seal. The universal seals, found in the grimoire, represent the attributes, quality, and sphere of activity for the entity summoned and it must react to the seal. The personal seals are ones made by the magician that must be accepted by the entities being worked with. I prefer the last approach for reasons I'll explain in more detail in the next lesson.

The sigil/seal is placed into the magic triangle, which acts as a gateway to the home plane of the entity. The magician also constructs a magical circle that could be used to protect themselves from the entity called forth. The protection is needed because it is summoned against its will and is usually constrained to do as the magician commands. The magician might call on yet other entities to help accomplish that task.

The other detail that needs to be attended to is the creation of a sustainable atmosphere for the entity. One reason Bardon lists for the magician creating the atmosphere, as opposed to letting the entity generate it, is that if the entity generates the atmosphere, it may put the magician entirely under its influence. A second reason is that most entities can't exist in this plane of reality without some medium to channel them. Incense is used in the traditional approach because it can embody the plane of existence the entity is in. The entity uses the smoke to assume a shape for the magician to interact with. We can think of the incense smoke as a medium which provides both smell, and a material for forming an appearance.

Traditional evocation involves ceremonial magic, which incorporates lots of props and tools. The ceremonial tools are mainly meant to help the magician reach a state of mind that allows them to successfully work the magic. As each tool represents a specific trigger in the consciousness, the activation of each trigger pushes the magician toward the ideal state of consciousness and empowerment that allows them to do the evocation.

The mindset of the magician is a vital factor for the success of evocations. Without a proper mindset the success of any act of magic will be sabotaged by the magician, creating a slingshot effect. The beliefs and expectations of a magician determine whether or not a given act of magic is successful. The use of ceremonial tools and other props comes second to the internal reality the magician is working with, though these tools serve to align and direct the mind toward the projected goal.

What's written above is an explanation of the fundamental dynamics of how traditional evocation works. It provides an essential grounding in the roots of evocation, though it's not necessary to use this approach for every evocation you do. In fact, I rarely use traditional evocation or the ceremonial tools. I dislike the concept of forcing entities to do my will, as I think that such constraints can only come back to haunt the magician down the line. I've mainly used this paradigm of evocation to understand the roots of where evocation came from. Aside from the issue I have with constraining an entity to do something against its will, I also find that one of the reasons traditional evocation doesn't work for me is that it involves having me be afraid of the entity. Fear is a saboteur, because it raises doubts in the mind and undermines the working.

When doing evocation, it's a good idea to consider why you are doing the evocation, and if the task you want the entity to perform can be accomplished another way. There will be certain types of tasks that are better suited to entities and certain ones that you should resolve yourself. I use evocation when I want the entity to perform an act that involves influencing a specific behavior or activity in my favor, but still leaves me with the actual decision. For example, one entity I work with is focused on making me aware of potential opportunities. I still have to choose to follow through on those opportunities, but the entity takes care of an essential task that I simply couldn't do. Its focus is on scanning space/time for the opportunities and then making me aware of them. It's not a skill I have, but it's a skill that entity has.

On the other hand, evoking an entity to do something you could handle yourself is wasteful and also keeps you from sharpening your own skills. It's important to recognize this distinction so that you can improve your skills. For example, I once wanted to buy a car. Instead of creating an entity, I did an enchantment to obtain the money I needed to purchase the car. I already had a job, but I knew I needed more money than I'd have available at short notice. By doing the enchantment, I was able to focus on very specific details the entity might not have considered. I realized I needed to attend to the task, instead of assigning it to an entity. It's a case of picking the right tool for the right job, and with evocation, it's better to have an entity do something you can't do, then have it do something you could've easily handled yourself.

In ceremonial magic, evocation is done with specific tools, incenses, and other props that are used to create a specific atmosphere that accommodates the entity as well as the altered state of mind the practitioner needs to be in to work with the entity. However, evocation can also be done with collages, paintings, and other techniques that are non-traditional but still enable the magician to make a connection with the entity. Although some magicians will claim that traditional approaches are more powerful, I've found that using more artistic approaches to evocation has been more successful for me. Evocation, much like any other magical technique, is really based on your understanding of the fundamental principles at work. If you understand those principles, you can personalize your approach to evocation using whatever tools best help you express that understanding to the entity and the world.

Evocation isn't limited to evoking entities. The magician can evoke another person or a past/future version of themselves. Just as with invocation, it ultimately comes down to connection, and understanding how to use evocation to create and embody a connection you want to manifest in the environment around you. I have successfully evoked people into my life, by using specific attributes as a way to create a connection with people who had those attributes. Evocation operates on the principle of connection and names. The name of an entity, or an attribute, or a person is a powerful tool that allows the magician to create a connection to the manifestation of the entity, attribute, or person. That connection is used to pull the entity or person into their life and to embody the attribute from within themselves in the external environment.

Evocation, like other techniques of magic, is customizable to a person's preferences, provided that person isn't deluding themselves. I've used modern media, non-traditional approaches to evocation, very successfully, right up to evoking my wife into my life (which is as physical a result as you can get!). I still use some ceremonial instruments because they do serve to aid and guide my consciousness to the state I need to be in to make the magic work, but I also find that the customization of my techniques firms up the subjective synthesis I'm working with. Some magicians may find that traditional evocation works for them. It may mirror the internal reality and perceptions they have of dealing with entities, and so be needed in order to deal with the beings they work with. But just because this approach works for some doesn't mean it works for everyone.

Psychological Evocation

Psychological evocation argues that the spirits that are worked with are wholly summoned from the subconscious mind of the magician. For instance, some magicians would argue that the goetic daimons are just psychological aspects of the mind that we've given a different figure and form so that we can work with them. By personifying these aspects as daimons we give them a medium to communicate with, as well as a way for us to gain power over them. All of the spirits are related to that central column of awareness and will, i.e. the ego of the person.

In the psychological paradigm, ceremonial magic might be used, but there are also other techniques. The writer or artist utilizes the media of writing, paint, or whatever form of expression is available to provide the psychological aspect a physical form by which it can be worked with. For example, the medium of clay could be sculpted to create a statue that represents the entity. Memes are another example of media which have taken on a life of their own.

The meme transmits a specific concept to a person, and also seeks to replicate itself as much as possible. Commercials are the most obvious forms of memes that re-present a company as well as the services of the company in a concrete form. The problem with the meme is that the technique relies far too much on other people to sustain its existence. The meme is only meaningful if people can understand it. Furthermore, the real power of the meme can only occur when people respond to it and evoke it into their behavior (for instance going out and buying fast food after seeing a fast food commercial). This evocation gives the energy within the meme a means of manifesting into reality and allows it to replicate.

I don't agree with the psychological paradigm for evocation. I think that a magician can work with aspects of themselves, and even do evocations of those aspects. I also think that arguing that every entity is a psychological aspect of you is solipsistic and quite problematic because it can lead to delusions. Many contemporary magicians, when confronted with a phenomenon that can't be explained in terms of psychology, get freaked out because they suddenly realize the universe is much larger than they thought. A psychological view of magic is unreliable because it attempts to explain everything away and in the process ends up creating a rather cynical perspective of magic. There's no mystery when you think you have everything figured out (at least until the mystery comes along and bites you in the ass). In addition, the purely psychological approach is concerned more with visualization and generating artificial states of emotion as a way of demonstrating the effects of evocation. However, these effects are more or less internal and as such fall into invocation, as opposed to evocation.

Once again, it's a matter of determining what works for you, but I'll admit that that I would take up traditional evocation before I utilized psychological evocation in dealing with entities. I do use painting and writing and other artistic mediums for my evocations, but I also know that I'm working with an entity that is just as real as I am. The psychological approach denies such an existence in favor of making it into either a psychological or symbolic aspect (i.e. the entity is just a symbolic representation of the attributes it represents). Still, it may work for some people. Knowing how you approach the world around you necessarily defines the techniques you use and how you conceive of the results that occur. If you use this paradigm or it makes the most sense to you, it may be what you need.

My Approach to Evocation

My approach to evocation as it applies to entities is one that's based on the principle that every being has its own distinct spirit. This approach could be called animistic, in that for me spirits can be in anything. For example, I personify my car, give it a name, and in doing so interact with the spiritual energy within it. Is that car now an entity? Some magicians will say yes, while others will say no. I fall into the yes camp. I think that anything can have a spirit and that it's very important to treat the spirits with respect and honor. The personal relationships I create are ones focused on working with the entities toward goals that are beneficial to all. I've found that this approach has been the most successful one for me. The entities I work with respond much more favorably if respected than if I try to force them to do something.

However this doesn't mean I worship them. I do daily prayers to some entities, but the majority of relationships I have aren't based on devotion or worship. Instead they're based on an acknowledgement of equality and a desire to work toward mutual ends. I also create entities, when I can't find an entity that suits my needs or just want to make one to deal with a very specific situation. The benefit of creating an entity as well is that there are some contemporary issues that we deal with that there are no existing entities for.

One of the benefits of creating an entity is that you can give it a physical residence to live in while you work with it. That residence could be as simple as the programming symbol you created for it, or it could be more complex. I put some of my entities into statues. My speed limit entity actually resides in a little medallion hung over the rear view mirror. The benefit of housing such entities is that they are given a permanent residence and as such don't need to be evoked every time you work with them. Because you program an entity when you create it, you also create the parameters by which it's activated, so it's never released in a situation where it's not appropriate for it to be there. Remember that you do need to feed an entity you've created. However, that detail isn't really different from evoking an entity, as usually to evoke it you have to provide the means for it to exist here. Feeding works on the same principle. Give the entity a means to sustain its existence so you can work with it.

My overall approach with any entity is to work with it in an equal partnership. Even with the entities I create I focus on creating a relationship where they get just as much out of the relationship as I do. I work with entities for several different reasons and in several different ways. The first reason is that sometimes I'm too emotionally invested in a situation to resolve it personally using magic. By creating or evoking an entity, I can allow it to handle the situation for me, without my personal biases interfering. I've used this approach in job hunting. By having an entity work on generating potential job opportunities for me, I can focus more on the applications, resumes, and interviews when they occur. The entity pushes potential job opportunities to my awareness, and then I apply for them. I also created my car entity to help me improve my driving and keep me from going over the speed limit. Again I chose to use an entity because I was too emotionally attached to the results and would have sabotaged my working if I had tried to attend to it personally.

Another reason I create or evoke entities is to learn something new. Because entities embody specific characteristics and attributes, they are ideal for teaching specific skills related to those qualities. I created a financial entity in 2006, after I realized I didn't know much about finances. Though I could manage money day to day, I didn't have a long term plan of action. The financial entity began to teach me about money, steering me toward buying particular books on finances, lecturing me about my attitude regarding money, helping to generate interest in my products at vending events (which thus brought in more money) and pushing me to write about my experiences, partially to educate others, but also to educate myself. It's fair to say that this entity was my teacher in the sense that it motivated me to learn more about finances and where I wanted to be in life. In another case, to learn more about divination and hone my divination skills, I worked with a pop culture entity, Miss Cleo. While the real Miss Cleo might have been a fake, the persona or entity of Miss Cleo was a being who could tap into all the energy being put toward it and so had some knowledge and power. By choosing to work with her, I learned how to improve my skills, and eventually was even pushed toward learning a lot more about space/time magic.

A final reason I create or evoke entities has to do with the fact that they exist in different dimensions and have different perceptions than I do. They can also provide intuitive flashes to help steer me in a specific direction that I might've missed otherwise. One of the first entities I created was a space/time entity called Cerontis, whose sole role is to make me aware of opportunities I might miss. He doesn't make those opportunities manifest--I do that. But he helps expand my awareness of opportunities. I have to admit I've found a lot more opportunities as a result of creating that entity, because I know he's always looking for them. In fact, when I programmed him, I incorporated his method of feeding into what he did for me. Every opportunity he presents to me also gives him energy to continue finding more opportunities. It creates a domino effect, one opportunity chaining into another, with him feeding from the opportunities, but also feeding them.

Evocation is a powerful technique. I think the reason my evocations have been successful is because I treat the entities I work with respect and equality. I've never had to command an entity or use the various levels of protection that other magicians feel they need to use. If anything by choosing to treat an entity with respect, my relationship with it has produced far more in the way of results than forcing it to comply with my desires. Remember that the mentality of traditional/medieval evocation came out of Christian fear of dealing with beings that didn't fit into the Christian metaphysical universe. If that mentality fits you, use it, but if it doesn't, take a different approach. I have, and as of yet in my dealings have not had any harm visited upon me.

Exercise

What is your approach to working with spirits or entities? How did you come to this approach and how effective has it been? What could you test about that approach or change?

Lesson 18: Evocation 2

In this lesson, we'll explore Evocation further in terms of how to use art, words, and other such tools for evocation purposes as well as discuss where evocation fits into the process of magic.

One key component of a successful evocation (according to several authors) is the use of incense as a way of creating a substance the entity could use to give itself form. Although I've done a fair amount of ceremonial magic, I'm not really a fan of getting lots of ingredients together to do a ritual. While in Seattle, I lived in a small cramped house and there wasn't a lot of room to put down a traditional circle, break out all the tools, and light the incense. And while I'd have loved to do a ritual in my backyard, somehow I don't think the neighbors would have appreciated it. For that matter I wouldn't really have appreciated explaining what I was doing, if the authorities had been called in to investigate.

At the same time, as I read these books, I'm told by at least one author that any evocation I do that isn't by the book is inauthentic and not a real evocation. So I'm left in a quandary. I want to evoke, but I don't have the physical space or materials and it's not authentic if I don't follow the instructions. And if I want to do an evocation to get help finding a better ritual space and proper materials, I'm kind of stuck. There's no allowance for experimentation here, is there? The answer to that question depends on the perception you cultivate about the magic you practice.

As it turns out there is room for experimentation and your evocations can be effective, even if you don't pursue the traditional route. The symbol does not make the reality, it just denotes it. If that's the case, and from my experiences it has been, then it's possible that it's not so much the particular act in and of itself that works, as it is what the act is supposed to do for all parties involved. If evocation is about creating a link and a space for an entity to use so that it can interact with this reality safely, then tools and the rest of a ceremonial ritual compose only one method among many that can be used to accomplish that task.

One evocation method involves taking several principles from Franz Bardon's work and applying it toward creating a gateway that allows the practitioner to evoke the entity, while at the same time keeping the entity safe so that it can interact with the magician. Bardon uses an approach called impregnation, where he puts into an object a specific meaning/energy that can then be evoked from that object. In the case of working with an entity, the magician would carve or put the seal/sigil (i.e. the symbol) of the entity on the object in question and use that symbol as a focus. The focus on the symbol impregnated the meaning, and access to the entity, into the talisman. Then the magician would evoke the entity, show it the talisman, and get it agree to using the talisman as a portal. After that the magician could use the talisman to evoke the entity whenever they pleased.

Another Franz Bardon technique involved using a magic mirror. The mirror is painted with the symbol of the entity, and then impregnated with the particular vibration or energy the entity identifies with. The mirror can then be used to evoke the entity, with it appearing in the mirror.

While I treat entities as real beings that exist in their own right, I also agree with Bardon's idea that the appearance of them is likely only a symbolic embodiment created to represent the particular power/vibration/concept being worked with. In other words, the entities are real, but they know that to effectively work with someone they need to interact with him/her in a way that makes sense and yet still accomplishes the goal at hand. This is one reason incense is used in traditional evocation. The smoke of the incense allows the entity to create a shape it can use to interact with the person. I like Bardon's approach better.

Along with Bardon's approaches I also use personalized symbols (based on the Alphabet of Desire technique developed by Austin Spare) with entities, to work with them. Bardon discusses three types of symbols that could be used to evoke an entity. A personalized symbol system emphasizes a personal relationship with the entity being evoked. It embodies and explores the growth of relationships and is more effective to use in evocation than using more universal symbols. Universal symbols are used by many magicians, which dilute the power and connection of those symbols. While it's true that attention and energy can invest a symbol with power, if many magicians *use* that symbol they are spreading that attention and energy out, diluting the power and taking away from the efficacy of the workings. A personalized symbol is one that only the magician who created it knows. The power and connection of the symbol isn't diluted, because while other people may see it, only the magician can access the meaning that is within it. Additionally, the relationship between the magician and entity works because it's based off the magician's personal parameters (as set in the symbol) as opposed to someone else's parameters.

My particular approach to evocation is a synthesis of Bardon's impregnation/mirror techniques and Spare's artistic work. I use water color paints or colored pencils to create a gateway/portal/mirror to the particular entity I want to work with. The landscape of the painting represents both the native environment and the particular vibration or energy of the entity. I paint the personalized symbol that represents that entity, incorporating it into a representation of the body of the entity I'm working with. This serves as a key to activate the gateway and allow access to the entity. It's useful for evocation because I can turn the portal on or off as needed, and as such the evocation can be performed at any time, without a lot of ritual involved. The initial ritual is the act of painting the gateway and activating it with the entity's blessing. I've also recently considered that another benefit of such an approach is that it allows you access to an entity or even a specific influence or energy such as an elemental or planetary energy in such a way that you can draw on that energy when needed for other ritual workings you want to do. For example, if you've created an evocation drawing or painting or sculpture that evokes the planetary energy of Jupiter, you can use that painting to evoke that energy anytime you do a wealth magic working. Simply open the gate to that energy and add it to the wealth magic working you are doing.

When I do my evocations, I usually touch the symbol and mentally call the entity to me. I know the entity has arrived when the painting "comes to life". The landscape and representation of the entity will seem to move as I look at it. I can then interact with the entity and do whatever magical working I've planned on. This form of evocation can be used with any sort of entity and as I mentioned above it can also be used with elemental, planetary, and other types of energy that aren't necessarily personified in the form of an entity.

Remember that entities embody only one form of interaction with a particular type of energy. In some ways, many entities can be thought of as personifications of a planetary or elemental energy, but a magician can work with a much more raw form. A painting enables that kind of working because it can be very abstract in what it presents, much like dealing with a raw elemental or planetary force. The painting will still channel the energy being worked with, but the magician works with that energy directly without having to rely on an intermediary.

I've also applied this concept of working with raw forces in evocation to dealing with personality aspects/emotional blockages of the self; I essentially evoke myself. I've painted several different versions of my internal landscape, complete with a symbol, and used them to evoke my internal personality aspects in order to work with them more closely, while dissolving energetic blockages. That approach has greatly helped me in that internal work, and allowed me to get to know parts of myself I don't consciously interact with otherwise. I find it useful to do a new painting every so often to reflect the changes in your psyche.

The evocation of the self can also be used as a snapshot of that particular moment in time that it was created and to my consciousness at that time. I evoke my past self using the painting and then instruct that self. I give him information that will allow him to organize his choices to make my current life easier. I imprint in the earlier self experiences that are yet to come, providing déjà vu and showing what not to do in that situation, in order to change the situation into a favorable outcome. In this way I can change my past by influencing the as of yet future actions of my past self. The déjà vu experiences I've had over the years have always been warnings about what not to do in specific situations and every time I haven't followed those warnings I've regretted it. The déjà vu experiences usually show me the result of an action taken that shouldn't be taken, so I have full warning and it's up to me to decide if I'll change that moment and avoid a problem I'd have experienced otherwise.

I suggest that evocation isn't such a strict discipline that creative innovations can't be used or invented to make this act more effective. To argue that a magical technique must be done only one way is to retard the evolution of magic. Treating entities like antagonists creates a dualistic Us vs. Them mindset with the accompanying tension sure to disrupt the evocation. Working with them as partners creates a lack of tension and a focus instead on meeting the goals at hand. Remember that the attitude and perception you adopt necessarily impact the subjective synthesis that is used when doing a magical working. Success in magic can be found by attending to the internal details so that when they affect your external workings, they do so in a favorable manner. An evocation will work for you provided that you know your subconscious and conscious emotions and work with them in a mindful manner, even as you approach what you evoke with respect.

Below is are two examples of evocation paintings I've done:

This is an evocation of the totem of Elephant. I created it to work with Elephant (in conjunction with several other entities) for space/time magic, but also to get to know Elephant better.

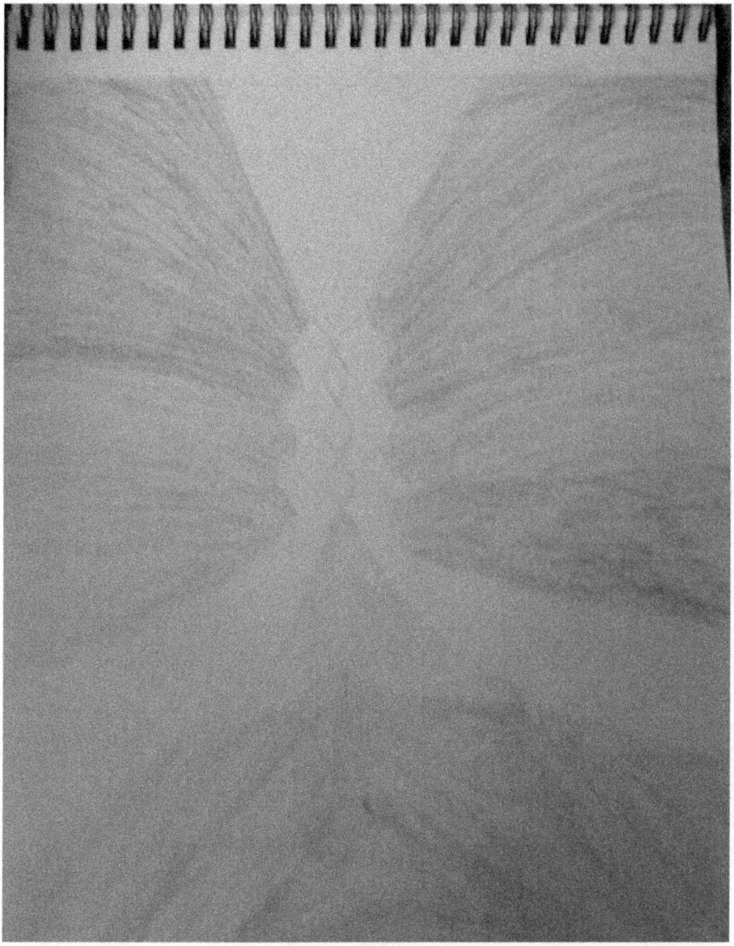

This is a planetary art drawing of the planetary energy of Jupiter. It's hung in business office and evoked for wealth magic and any business dealings I have.

The Role of Evocation in the Process of Magic

Much like invocation, evocation can either be a singular technique in your process of magic, or one used in conjunction with other techniques of magic. I rarely use just evocation in a magical working. I typically treat an evocation as an enhancer of other magical workings I'm doing, but it's also fair to say that an evocation can be effective on its own in your magical process. As I mentioned in an earlier lesson, it's worthwhile to consider this kind of technique useful for situations where you are too close to the issue that needs to be resolved, but as can also be seen in this lesson, using evocation to channel particular types of influences is also useful.

Exercise:

How would you use evocation in your magical process? What might you do differently as a result of these lessons?

Lesson 19: Divination and the Process of Magic

I have to admit that I'm fairly skeptical when it comes to divination, specifically the use of it in magical work. You might wonder then why I've included it in the Process of Magic course. The reason is that a lot of people use divination for their magical work, and clearly there is some use for the various divinatory techniques or people wouldn't use them. I suppose where I differ from the textbook advice on divination is that I don't do a divination before doing a magical working. In many books you'll find that divination is advised before performing a magical ritual to determine how successful the ritual will be as well as examining other consequences that might occur. Thus it could be argued that divination is a technique that should show up in your process of magic. So why doesn't it show up in mine?

There's a couple reasons I don't employ divination in a working. One reason is based off the principle of observation, which is that the very act of observation alters what is being observed. How this applies to divination is if you are getting ready to do a working and you do a divination that suggests something negative will occur, the chances that something negative will occur multiply because the act of observation via divination sets up or foreshadows that act. One might point out that the point of divination is to "show" the future, but I'd argue that all divination really does is present possibilities of what might occur. Nonetheless it doesn't show all the possibilities that could occur (your average divination technique can't do this because you are working with a limited medium which can only show so much). So rather than relying on a technique to tell me if my working will succeed or not, I simply do the working.

In fact, simply doing the working is the second reason I don't use divination before a magical working. I figure that doing a divination has one hidden block many people don't consider: You doubt your own power. If you feel the need to do a magical working to address a situation, then trust in that working. If you are concerned about consequences, plan for those consequences in your magical working. You'll have to deal with the situation one way or another, so it's better to simply do the working and resolve the situation. Trust in your power, and in your wisdom to use that power for good effect.

Those are my reasons and your mileage may vary. If you find that doing a divination before a magical working is essential then do it. Or try it one time without a divination and see if there's a noticeable difference and make a decision based off your findings.

So is there a point to divination? A typical reason a person chooses to do divination is to obtain information about a specific situation in the present or the future (though it can also be applied to the past). At one point in time I would do a divination for the year, pulling a tarot card out for each month and writing the information in my journal. I'd find that each month seemed to adhere to the reading I'd gotten, but I began to wonder if the reason for that was self-fulfilled prophecy. In other words I picked a card out and wrote the meaning down for a given month and when the month came around I started looking for the expected outcome I'd associated with the month when I did the reading. I realized that if I wanted divination to be more effective, I needed to develop a way of doing divination that showed me multiple possibilities. I also accepted that any divination system is still going to be inherently limited because you are still getting a filtered perspective via the cards. What I present below are some of the divination methods I've developed over the years that I've found useful for obtaining information about multiple outcomes using tarot cards. I suspect these could be applied to other divination tools as well. In the next lesson I'll cover how I've used divination tools such as Tarot for enchantments.

Perhaps part of the problem with divination is that it might be considered a rather passive form of magic: I put some cards down and suddenly I know the future that *will happen to me*. However, I have found that divination can be a very active form of magic that *I make happen*. You have to do a lot of interpretation, and be open to a lot of possibilities in regards to the interpretation.

What actually occurs when a divination is done is not so much a foreseeing of the future, but rather a person choosing to perceive one or two specific probabilities from a field of infinite probabilities. The problem mainly comes down to the person choosing to believe in just one probability, as opposed to exploring other probabilities of the future that could be just as useful to them, if they were willing to question what they perceive about their probabilities and the future. In addition, they give too much authority to the people who tell the "future", thereby giving away their responsibility and choices.

Meaning is interconnected with events. I would argue, though, that *it is your placement of meaning on an event that creates the probabilities that spread from it.* This occurs due to the nature of investing meaning into the event. When you do this, you impose your own biases, subjectivities, etc., on that event. These biases shape the event, change it, and bring out certain possibilities that are more likely to occur, while putting other possibilities in the background, making them less likely to occur. The following example illustrates this principle.

If you have a fiery temper, and someone insults you, what is the most likely possibility that will occur? Will you hit that person, or insult the person back? Or will you just walk away? As you think this over, consider that if you have a fiery temper, it will have an effect on which possibilities will more or less likely manifest. Now add in other factors that could affect this situation for you. Is this person a total stranger? Is this person a friend you know, who's not so much insulting you as greeting you? Is this person a hated enemy? All of these factors, these meanings you read into the event, affect it and determine the probabilities that will happen. Of course, the other person also brings his/her own meanings into the events, and this likewise affects the possibilities that manifest into reality. Meaning is also connected to synchronicity. The meaning we place into random coincidences, arguing that these incidents happened for a reason, is called synchronicity. We link these events to ourselves, to other people and events, and use them to justify why such events occur.

As I briefly mentioned above, when referring to how people will believe in one possible future, and thus block out other probabilities, belief is the key to the temple of divination. Belief in what you do is integral to making the magic work, but sometimes belief can hinder more than it helps. And in the case of the tarot, where the stereotype of being able to read the future has become so pervasive, belief is much more of a hindrance than a help, unless you are willing to change the belief about the supposed reality of a situation. What you must remember is that beliefs can be changed, and the more malleable you are with your beliefs, the better you are at working magic effectively. Occasionally, it can be useful to believe that the tarot has predicted a specific future, but the reading has to be exceedingly specific to iron out the random factors that can change the probability, so that, while it may occur, the probable future doesn't happen the way you expect.

In other words, we can't cling to beliefs too strongly, or they will dictate our reality. The true power of a magician is in knowing how to change reality to suit his/her needs. Accordingly, we must be wary of any stereotypes that reinforce a belief about a tool of magic. And being willing to change a belief at the drop of a hat certainly doesn't hurt either.

Even with the recognition that the tarot can represent more than one or two futures, you must still be wary of mistaking the tool for the actual practice. Learning to work space/time magic ultimately is done through the magician. The tarot serves as a tool, as an expression of the magician, but precisely because it can limit your scope of possibilities by predicting a limited number of probabilities, you have to be willing to explore alternative avenues of space/time magic. This applies to any tool of divination.

Before you explore those other avenues, there are some methods you can use with tarot cards or other divinatory tools that can be useful for fleshing out probabilities. These methods are also useful for beginning to explore a non-linear frame of mind.

First, I suggest that the tarot cards you use should have a lot of diverse imagery on them. To give you an example, I use the Voyager tarot deck, the elemental hexagon deck, and the Alchemy Deck by Ray Buckland. Each of these decks provides a variety of symbolism that can be useful for representing diverse probabilities.

I also suggest not memorizing the meanings of the cards. I've found that the best readings occur through my intuition. You should seek the intuitive impact of the cards, as opposed to a more cerebral understanding of the meanings behind them. In other words, what do the cards tell YOU? When you focus on memorizing the meanings, you're focusing on the words that describe the experiences the cards give you. But can those words alone really tell you the meaning of the cards, or instead can you rely on your intuition of the imagery, choosing to explain the experience through the medium of the words you choose, as opposed to what someone else dictates to you? If you feel that you do need to rely on more classical interpretations of the cards, you may find it useful to do extensive pathworking with each card, in order to let it teach you the meanings behind it. After that, you'll understand the cards better, because you'll have personally experienced the meanings and symbolism of each card.

Primarily, you should learn to "listen" to the cards. I always shuffle my cards until I get the message from them (or perhaps from my intuition), to stop shuffling and start laying out the spread. Remember, when you see the cards, that they do not depict the future, past, or present. They can give you suggestions of what *might be*, but nothing is fixed or determined, unless you are willing to invest the energy into what you perceive. I find that by perceiving the cards as giving suggestions, as opposed to dictating a specific future, that I am much more open to alternate probabilities that might not be shown in the cards, but nonetheless can still occur, and thus have an effect on the situation being examined. You may also note that I mentioned past and present. I always find it's best to consider that there are multiple presents and pasts, as opposed to an unchangeable singular past/present. Psychology has shown that many of our memories of the past are "made up" by the brain, which for me suggests some bleed-over of alternate past probabilities.

The first method I like to use is one in which I draw one card for the past, one for the present, and three for the future. These five cards are merely the start of the reading, however. If you want details or alternate probabilities, simply continue pulling cards intuitively out of the deck. This can include any part of the deck, not just the top card. As you look at the cards, write down the impressions you get, focusing on being as specific as possible, but also allowing the raw data to express itself as it will for you. You may even find that instead of writing, you draw something. The idea is to follow your intuition, allowing it to tell you what you need to know. When you look at the cards, try to consider as well not merely the initial meaning, but any alternate meanings that spring to mind, for either a single card, or for a group of cards. Key yourself into finding more than one probability, considering the cards from more than one perspective. Also, ask yourself how well the cards depict the situation. Do you know of any factors that are not presented in the cards? If so, how do those factors affect the probabilities that the cards depict?

Another spread I use is based on the eight arrows of chaos from chaos magic. One card is in the center, representing the untapped potential of the situation, the impetus to make the situation happen. Eight cards are spread outward representing not just eight individual possibilities, but multiple possibilities, all connected to each other and to the potential impetus. I visualize cords of energy connecting each card to all the other cards in the spread. You can do this with a traditional spread as well. The goal is not just to read the cards, but to interact with them, starting with the card that represents the drive to manifest change.

For the potential impetus in the center (or wherever you would place a significator in your spread), I usually use the Magician card (although you can use any card that best represents the impetus for your working), representing as it does, for me, action or desired action via magic. But that's my preference. On the impetus card I place a piece of paper with my own personal sigil on it, representing my force bonded with that of all the possibilities of the Magician. I usually spend some time meditating or pathworking with the Magician beforehand, so as to get a feel for how the personality of the Magician card meshes with my own.

For me, the Magician is a guide, and each card is a doorway that leads not to one meaning, but to many. These doorways can also lead to each other, because every possibility is related, even if that relationship is one of opposition. You might have realized that eight cards, plus the impetus card, involves a fair amount of pathworking, and you are quite right. It does. This is why my method is different from a standard reading. The process of making the possibility manifest happens through the pathworking done with the cards. You explore as many different avenues of possibility as you feel you need to. And, of course, you can always bring more cards to your circle. The real question is how much detail you want to cover.

I tend to be fairly detailed, so I'll sometimes include extra cards, or instead focus on soaking in as much detail for the pathworking that I'm doing. I'm also always willing to extend such workings through a period of days. You're not reading a future so much as actualizing a possibility or possibilities. I don't set a specific time period for a ritual such as this, but I will give it as much time as I need to be sure of the details. I know that in the process of the pathworking I'm doing, I refine and shape the probabilities. I explore probabilities I don't want to manifest, and turn them into free energy, which I pour into the other possibilities until I actively arrive at the "future" I want to create, aware, at the same time, of other possibilities that can either help or hinder that "future."

When I'm pathworking, I pay close attention to the card's symbolism. For each card, I take the symbolism I find, and impose a sigil on the doorway of the card. You can physically draw a sigil and place it on the card, or you can mentally visualize it, which is what I usually do. Either method will work. I destroy the sigils that represent the possibilities I don't need, either burning the physical representations or mentally tearing down the door, and then putting the energy toward the probabilities I want to manifest, charging up the sigils that represent the potential realities.

As you can see, this technique focuses on working actively with the cards to produce more than one possibility, to achieve perspective, and then push that perspective toward manifestation. Even if you just want to manifest one specific future, it's still important to discover and explore alternate probabilities. By doing so, you achieve a far better understanding of the magic you do and the choice you are making. Nothing is determined that we cannot ourselves determine, but gathering information helps you decide what possibility is most useful for you. The more aware you are of a variety of possibilities, the less trapped you are in linear time. Through doorways of possibilities, you find the keys to your own empowerment, the achievement of your own realities, the emancipation of your own life from that which seeks to keep you trapped: the dull, boring reality of the mainstream that insists in absolutes to keep you in your "place."

I suggest that you meditate on one card for while, take a break for a few minutes, and then move onto the next card. By taking a break you give yourself a chance to ground and digest what you've already taken in. Each time, after you've meditated on each card, write down your experiences in a journal so that you can look at what you've written at a later time. I've always found my writings to be highly useful in making sense of what I've meditated about, and also in understanding situations that later occurred as the cards "predicted." Remember, though, to keep yourself open to other probabilities and perspectives.

Free Form Spreads and Dual-Deck Readings

When I have used Tarot for divination readings, I use freeform spreads in my readings, instead of standard readings. One of the reasons I suspect divination readings can be problematic has to do with the actual spread. Different spreads have associated meanings with them. These meanings bias the reader in regards to the overall reading, because they set certain standards into the reading. My way of getting around this issue, both for myself and other people I do readings for, is to do free form spreads, which means the spread can and will change and isn't regulated to a set number of cards. The placement of the cards in the spread is done intuitively with this approach, as opposed to using a rote formula for the spread. The benefit of the intuitive placement of the cards is that any meaning associated with the placement of the cards is solely derived from the reader. This filters out biases that traditional spreads would otherwise introduce into the reading.

The reason the cards aren't limited to a specific number is to allow for better exposure of the intuitive possibilities that are present in the reading. More detail is allowed into the reading, which opens the magician to the perception of more possibilities. The cards will still modify each other because they have a relationship to each other, but the person can get further details as needed instead of relying on a limited spread, with limited information.

Another modification I've made to divination reading is using two tarot decks instead of one. Calyxa Omphalos, who created the Elemental Hexagon deck, told me about this concept of using two tarot decks to do readings at Pantheacon. She uses the Elemental Hexagon Deck and Buckland's Alchemy deck. For her, the elemental hexagon deck represents nouns: people, places, things, etc., while Buckland's alchemy deck represents verbs. It's essentially sentence diagramming via tarot and that in and of itself is intriguing, but I choose to go a different route when using the dual deck system.

I also used the elemental hexagon deck and Buckland's alchemy deck. In my system, the elemental hexagon cards are spatial cards. They can represent people, places, and things, but more importantly they represent the actual space those people, place and things embody.

The alchemy deck are the connector cards. The connector cards represent temporal influences that move through the spatial cards and carry the influence of each space to other spaces. Remember that time denotes movement and for any node to have connection to another node, there needs to be an element of time. Connector cards also represent emotions and conceptual meaning. Emotions and conceptual meanings are what motivate changes in spatial cards and as such they are included as temporal influences, because of the actions they can cause. The connector cards seem to enhance the spatial cards, because they provide complementary information about what is acting on a given space.

When picking out two tarot decks to use for dual deck readings, it's worthwhile to use decks that have related themes. The elemental hexagon deck uses the elements of the periodic table, which meshes well with the theme of alchemy in Buckland's cards. You don't necessarily need to use these decks to do the dual deck readings, but finding decks that have related themes will likely increase the effectiveness of the reading, because of how the decks will work with each other. I think tarot decks reflect the personality of the people who devised them, but also are representative of the beings depicted on the cards. It's important to recognize this, in order to use two decks that complement each other.

When using the dual deck system for divination, one way to modify the reading is to treat the spatial cards as open and closed spaces (See pictures below). If the connector card is bring a negative space into your life, closing that space closes the influence of the card. This is done by changing the direction that the spatial card faces. Obviously, with such a reading a person will need to make changes in his/her life, but this act can start the necessary impetus in the subconscious of the person, planting that seed for change that removes the negative influence from your life. It's another way to use the dual deck system, and what makes it so effective is that by having one set represent connectors and one set represent influences, places, people, etc., you can effectively use the system to change those influences in your life.

Custom spreads and using a dual deck system can open the magician up to a variety of perspectives and possibilities in the reading. I've found it's produced accurate readings with clients, as well as for my own circumstances. However, Tarot isn't just for divination. I've found it to be a very effective tool for enchantment, and even for invocations and evocations.

Figure one: Open Spatial card on the right influencing the spatial card on the left via the connector card

Figure Two: The spatial card on the right is closed, closing off the power flow to the left card.

Exercise:

If you use some type of divination system such as tarot or runes, I'd like you to use it in an enchantment working such as I described above and then write down what you discovered when you used the divination system in that way.

Lesson 20: Enchantment and the Process of Magic

Enchantment is the direct practical application of magic to reality, as done by the magician, as opposed to a proxy such as an entity. That difference is important to note, because when a person does an enchantment, they are personally doing the magical work to achieve a result, whereas working with an entity via invocation or evocation, involves the entity doing the majority of the magical work.

Enchantment is different from divination in that we don't seek information. We seek results and we have decided to apply magic to achieve those results. Enchantment comes in many different techniques, but the essential reality of those techniques is that they are enchantments. The act of enchantment is the manifestation of a specific possibility into reality. An enchantment could be a spell, a sigil, a collage, or a number of other techniques, and the main difference is the form of the technique, as opposed to the underlying magical dynamic that informs the use of that technique.

Why Enchantments Fail

The reason an enchantment fails is a lack of understanding about the specific principles it is meant to access. This is why, in particular, spells are notorious for not being reliable. If you pick up your average spell book mostly what you find is a recipe like instruction book with ingredients and instructions on how to use ingredients to perform the spell. While this works just fine with actual cook book recipes, it's not quite so simple with spell books. In a recipe, you only need to follow the instructions to cook food without really needing to understand why the food is cook or how it is cooked. With magic, it's different. You are engaged in act of transformation much more profound than simply cooking food. If you don't understand the underlying principle of the spell: specifically how it will work and what it will do, it won't necessarily work. Magic, as a comprehensive process, is based in part on your ability to understand exactly what you are doing to alter reality.

You might say, "But I've used a spell and it worked." And it did, but the reason it did had more to do with your understanding of what the spell was going to do, as opposed to the actual spell itself. You applied that understanding to the spell when you chose to do it and you ended up with a result. It is your ability to conceptually understand how the magic will work that allows it to work. So for example, if you did a love spell, you had an idea of how that spell would work, which helped you frame the underlying principles involved. The problem is that this is a clumsy approach, and unfortunately most spells book don't explore in depth why a specific spell will work or what is actually happening when you use those various components to make the magical work happen. The author knows how the underlying principles work (if they actually created the spell), but if they don't explain it, it's left up to the reader to guess.

This is why I advocate for personalization of your magical work. Instead of relying on what worked for someone else, create your own version and use that. Obviously it does help if you have a foundation of work and experience to draw on, but the mark of a true magician is that they are able to personalize their own magical work by using what is most effective for them. The simple truth is that while magic has a process and principles that inform how it works, the techniques are malleable forms. There is a lot of flexibility when it comes to magical techniques because the techniques are used as interfaces to help the magician interact with the principles of magic. Thus, for example, why pop culture can be effectively integrated into magical work.

I'm going to share some of my personalized approaches to enchantments, to demonstrate how I've personalized the work. You are welcome to use my approaches, but as I advocate in my books and here, in the end it is better for you to personalize your magical work.

Using the Dual-Deck System for Enchantment

In the previous lesson I discussed the dual deck system. I've also used it for enchantment workings. For an example, see the picture below, which shows a short arm on the left and a long arm on the right. The card between the two arms is the core issue card. The left hand arm represents the enchantment to control and mitigate negative influences that would affect the desired result adversely. The right arm represents the desired outcome as well as specific node points and influence factors that are drawn on in order to make the desired result manifest into reality. The three nodal points that spread out from the right arm are the specific spheres of influence to be drawn on, with the connectors representing the best possible avenues to manifest those influences into the actual desired result.

Not all enchantments would need to be conducted this way, but for this instance it has been useful to approach it with an eye toward mitigating undesired influences. The dual deck system is useful because it provides visual symbols that can be manipulated physically, which the person can use to also manipulate possibilities in imaginary time. The cards provide an interface for the possibilities to manifest from, while making sense to the person doing the action, because the conceptualization of the possibilities is mediated through the cards and the maneuvering of them into specific spaces.

Intuition is also a useful component for this process, as a way of accessing imaginary time. Intuition is used in the placement of each nodal point as well as in the placement of the best connector for each nodal point. On the imaginary time level, intuition is used to match the possibilities to the nodal points and connectors, and help the person establish a meaningful connection between the reading and the events the person is influencing via the enchantment of the reading.

It's useful, with enchantment, to recognize that what is being worked with is the placement of a specific possibility into an existing system, in order to turn that possibility into reality and make it an inherent part of the system. Each nodal point represents a specific conceptual space within the system. The connectors (in reference to the picture above) represent emotional states of being that are key influences for realizing the impact of the conceptual spaces on the desired result. Since we want the positive conceptual spaces to have maximum impact, in order to ensure that the desired result becomes reality, we need to use connectors that will embody the path of least resistance and maximum empowerment of the desired result.

Connectors don't have to represent emotional influences. They can also represent the movement of time through spatial realities. Time is action and movement, what people are doing in a given space, or how that space is being used and worked with. Time changes space, but space provides the necessary place for that change to occur. The nodes represent spaces, and in this case space isn't just a physical location such as house or a city, but it can also be a person or thing. Space and time are conjoined, in the sense that you can't have one without the other. For space to change, time must flow through it, but time needs a spatial agent to act on, and to be utilized by. The dual deck represents this understanding and can be used for space/time magical workings.

Sigil work

My approach to sigil work typically has involved writing a statement of desire, getting rid of the repeating letters, and taking the remaining letters and turning them into a symbol. I've also used Austin Spare's technique of automatic drawing to just draw a sigil that represents the desire I want to manifest. Where I differ from typical approaches to sigil work is that I tend to utilize multiple sigils together. For example, this excerpt from my book Space/Time Magic demonstrates how I've used multiple sigils together via the medium of comic panels.

The essential idea is to use the comic book panels as representations of probabilities you want to imprint on space/time magic. The way panels work in comics is that one panel represents one moment of space/time in the story being told. For the story to proceed, the reader has to visualize the action occurring as he/she reads the comic. The gap between the panels, which is called the gutter, is where the visualization occurs. Essentially, the gap serves as a link from one panel to another. You visualize the action, the energy, everything that is needed to change one moment into another. The gutter, while seemingly empty, is the matrix in which two separate panels are transformed by the perception into a progression of events. With this understanding of how panels work, it's also possible to apply that understanding to the technique of using panels in magical workings.

The panel serves as the medium for imprinting the magician's will on space/time, and worked properly, can bring multiple probabilities into reality at once. You do this by using more than one panel representing multiple probabilities, no matter how improbable. And instead of exerting a lot of effort to bring that one probability into reality, you use the panels to link each probability to the other, so that when one probability becomes reality, the others are also brought into reality. Think of whatever number of situations you have that you would like to have manifest. Now draw however many rectangular panels you need to represent them. In each panel draw a sigil that represents an individual probability. Afterwards, draw lines between the panels, connecting the sigils, with the understanding that when one sigil comes into reality, others it is connected to will also come into reality. You can draw the lines so they go in multiple directions, instead of just going in one direction. With the lines, be creative with colors. Use colors that create a strong sense of meaning and connection for you. The challenging part comes when you're done with all the artwork. This is when you visualize all of the sigils together, and all of their purposes, as you charge them all at once. The key, if you choose to do that, is to keep the sigils firmly visualized as you charge them and distribute every bit of energy equally into each. This can be a bit exhausting to do in one sitting. But it can be done, and the lines that you draw between the panels help with that process. Visualize the energy spreading through the lines, into the panels, and onto the sigils.

You can also charge the sigils one at a time. What I do in this case is focus on the first panel, charging the sigil up and visualizing the energy going into the next panel. The next day I visualize the first sigil again, charging it up, but then visualize the next sigil and charge that up as well, particularly focusing on the energy going from one panel to the next. I do this with subsequent sigils in the series, and when all of them are charged accordingly, I destroy them as I see fit, or keep them, if that suits the nature of the work I wish to do with them, as one can charge sigils again and again, as needed. In any case, charging the sigils doesn't have to be hard.

Nor do the concepts of each sigil have to relate to the other sigils. Each one can deal with completely unrelated situations. The concept of this technique is to free the magician from linear time. The best aspect about it is that when one sigilized probability becomes reality, the other sigils are activated, and those probabilities become reality as well. In this way, you can address multiple situations with one technique.

Of course, this technique can easily be modified so that if you want certain sigilized probabilities to occur later than others you can do that, or even perform retroactive magic through this technique, setting it up so that when one sigil is activated for the present, other sigils will affect the past. It all depends on what you decide to build into the working. However, when I charge a lot of sigils, I have found it takes longer for them to manifest into reality. They become time delayed, activating only when the peak of energy is reached, and this can take longer than would occur with a single sigil. But the advantage to this technique is that the overall energy being used to manifest these sigils into reality is much more cumulative than that which occurs for a single sigil, the sigils draw each other into reality. Sometimes you sacrifice speed for strength, and with this technique I find that, though the speed of the manifestation is slow, the strength behind the probabilities makes it much easier to manifest probabilities that seem like they will only remotely manifest into reality.

As an example of this principle at work, in September 2003, I did a panel sigil working for a car, as well as the neutralization of a problematic situation with a colleague that had occurred. In April 2004, both situations resolved themselves. It took eight months for the results to manifest, but when they manifested, not only did I get the kind of car I needed – a reliable used car, which needed only minimal repair - but the problematic situation resolved itself in such a way as to ensure that the situation would never happen again. The energy and conditions for favorable materialization of probability had to be built up, but when they were, the probabilities manifested exactly when needed, and not a moment later.

You don't have to only use comic book panels. I like to paint in the watercolor medium. But instead of creating panels to paint in (though each painting can be a panel in and of itself, so you could do multiple sigil paintings and link them together with pushpins), I like to paint a central sigil that represents the main concept I'm working, and then from there paint other sigils, until the painting becomes a single large sigil containing multiple others within it. I charge both types of sigils by leaving them out where people can look at them. I find that the more attention they get, the more power they receive. The sigils are fired when I forget about what they mean. Instead of burning the sigils, I detach myself from their meaning, leaving the paintings or panels around me, but thinking of them as only scenery, something to occasionally admire. I've found that this method of firing the sigils has worked really well for me.

Collage Enchantments

Another of my favorite techniques to enchantments involves collages. I've always been a fan of William S. Burroughs and the cut-up technique where you cut random images and words and reassemble them into new messages. I view my scissors as blades that cut previous meanings from words and images, the paper as a blank canvas of reality waiting to be rewritten, and the glue as the ejaculate of possibility bonding the words and images into new meanings that describe an altered reality where a desired possibility is manifested. When I do this kind of enchantment, I usually enter into a flow state of mind (psychological state of creativity) and allow my intuition to take over, both in terms of cutting and gluing everything together. I've found consistent results using this kind of enchantment.

Writing Enchantments

Aside from writing statements of desire and turning them into sigils, I've also used writing itself as an enchantment. For instance, in my early twenties, I'd pick a theme for a chapter about my life, in the title, and then write about that theme, and use it as a way to write that theme into my life. I found that writing allowed me to fully express how a particular reality should manifest. Even my books are examples of that in that the act of writing them manifested specific experiences into my life to add to the books. The reason it works is because when I'm writing I enter a state of mind that allows me to access possibilities and with the act of writing I begin to bring them into reality. Never underestimate the power of simply providing a possibility a physical form of expression. Writing, painting, etc, all provide the expression of the possibility and through that physical expression provide a connection between reality and possibility so that the possibility can merge into and become part of reality.

Final Thoughts

I could provide more examples of enchantments, but hopefully you get my point about personalization. I've chosen to pursue mostly artistic expressions of enchantment workings and I've found it to be very useful because it's a medium I am gifted in. You might find other mediums more conducive to your enchantment workings. The medium isn't what matters, so much as what matters is that the medium allows you to express the possibility you want to bring into reality as well as allowing you to access the principles of magic that will aid in that manifestation.

Exercise

Create an enchantment of your own. What mediums did you use? How did those mediums allow you to connect to the principles of magic? How did the enchantment help you understand and apply the desired result to reality?

Lesson 21 Astral Projection and the Process of Magic

Astral projection involves the projection of your spirit into the astral plane(s), which is considered to be a plane of existence that isn't real in the way physical reality is, but allows people to work with the substance of the astral plane in a much more malleable away. There are several techniques that can be used to access the astral plane.

Your typical astral projection technique involves visualization of some sort. Usually you visualize yourself coming out of your body and accessing the astral plane. When you first project out of your body, you might see it near you or you might find your awareness in a different locale. The problem with this kind of technique is that if you can't visualize it makes hard to astral project. People who can visualize effectively won't have a problem visualizing themselves leaving their body, though it can also help to do this kind of work when you are in a meditative state or by self-hypnotizing yourself (to self-hypnotize yourself refer to the lesson on meditation).

However if you're the kind of person who has trouble visualizing, you may find a more tactile approach useful. Instead of visualizing, focus on a tactile sensation. One technique that Robert Bruce has written above involves feeling the end of rope in your chest, and tactilely pulling yourself out of your body.

I've found that this technique is very effective for achieving the out of body experience and typically once that hurtle is overcome it is easier to visualize the astral planes.

Astral projection is one of the skills of magic where you'll find differing perspectives on what the astral planes are and what purpose they represent. The astral plane is usually depicted in terms of duality, of good vs. evil or lower vs. higher planes of existence. It's not surprising that dualism is prevalent in how people conceive of the astral plane, when we consider the cultural beliefs that many people have been raised with. Dualism is found in many world mythologies and religious paths. The Christian religion has heaven and hell, while shamanic beliefs have versions of the upper and lower worlds and Norse mythology provides Valhalla and Hel.

This perspective also maintains that the astral plane is a linear spatial reality, attempting to "place" parts of the astral either lower or higher in relation to each other. The problem with this assumption is that it's primarily based on a cultural perception of what the afterlife might be, with the astral plane representing the gateway to other planes of existence. The various levels and sublevels of the astral plane, where different influences and polarities reside, seem to come more from the cultural imagination than actual reality. In fact the astral plane is a medium shaped by the information, media, etc., that we project into it. I'd argue that the astral plane isn't so much a gateway to other planes of existence as to the mass human consciousness and how that cultural consciousness perceives spiritual reality. Various attributes are often associated with the astral plane, including the division of the upper and lower planes. The upper plane is connected with guided meditation, lucid dreaming, the common arrival place, and also a place of positive energy. The lower astral planes are places of negative desires, vampiric forces, and nightmares. The attributes that are listed are ones we all experience. They aren't exclusive to the astral reality, though they could partially be derived from it, if the astral plane is based on the consciousness of people *and* other entities. However, whether the astral plane is seven layers or not and whether it's good on top and bad on bottom is something we need to question critically in order to determine what we can and can't get out of working with the astral.

When I initially experimented with astral projection I did encounter these lower and higher planes of the astral. But after a time I realized that this was just a convenient paradigm created by humans to explain the astral plane. They expected it to have seven layers and to be neatly divided into realms of good or bad influences, so that's what they saw. What was never questioned was whether this depiction of the astral plane was accurate. I began to wonder how an alien or an animal or someone from a different culture might experience the same place. I suspect that what really shapes the astral plane isn't just our consciousness, but also the impact of cultural consciousness which creates this subconscious belief in good vs. evil that has been hammered into us for two-thousand-plus years.

We can create/shape the astral realm we experience. Now it's true that we will still share this astral realm with other beings (with their perceptions of its reality), but my point here is that the paradigm we apply to it doesn't have to be the dualistic model mentioned above. The astral plane is a very flexible reality that can, to a degree, be shaped by the consciousness of the practitioner. I also suspect that if the majority of the people in the West stopped believing in the dualistic good vs. evil the astral plane would change to reflect the new cultural beliefs that were prevalent.

Other people who practice astral projection have realized this. Sylvan Muldoon is one such example. His approach to astral projection was rigorous and scientific, as opposed to the new age perspective. He acknowledged it could happen and had it happen to him frequently, but he found that the astral plane was different for different people, noting that everything in the astral plane comes from the mind of the projector. The dualistic model espoused by so many people is just that--a model. Approaching dualism as an objective representation simply doesn't reflect the myriad experiences that people have had. Rather, it only reflects the experiences that some people have as a result of applying cultural expectations to the astral plane, whether consciously or subconsciously.

What these various experiences suggest is that people have different concepts of what the astral plane is. We need to be wary of any person who claims to "know" what the astral is or embodies. They are, at best, describing their own model, as well as the social and cultural conditioning they've been raised with. These models may work or even fit into a particular magical system, but they shouldn't be mistaken as objective reality. Whatever the objective reality of the astral plane is, we experience it through our own subjective perceptions. In a way, we are responsible for creating the astral plane with our thoughts and preconceived notions about reality in general. We need to examine the models we apply to understand how our own motivations and fears are projected into the astral plane. That way when we encounter these projections we can consciously face them and choose to keep them or banish them as needed. I suspect that many of the so-called psychic attacks that occur on the astral plane come from the projector's subconscious mind. With conscious realization of that, the projector can dismiss or confront the subconscious issue for what it is and then move on to the original purpose of the projection.

You are responsible for the astral realm you project into (for the most part). By being aware of this you can fashion your own models to project into. In fact, the reason there are so many versions of the guided meditation is that each person can and will likely shape an internal or astral reality with what they are interacting with as a paradigm and/or spiritual reality at the time the guided journey is occurring. For instance, my favorite model to project into is a rising spiral of DNA, with access to other planes of existence on each point on the DNA ladder. I find this model the most useful because DNA and genetics currently intrigue me, but also because I think of the universe as a giant DNA helix. Another model I've used in the past has been a hallway of doors to different parts of what I've perceived as the astral. Sometimes this hallway has also led me to explore other planes of existence outside the astral. Again this is a model I've superimposed on the astral planes for my own use. Other people undoubtedly have their own models as well.

A good example of that would be the work of Robert Bruce who argues that the astral planes are a generation of the universal consciousness. Yet he also acknowledges that *perception* varies from person to person. We aren't limited to one universal model, but rather the astral realms we experience are ones that we at least in part help to create. Bruce's model for the astral realm is a complex, multilayered, energetically generated dimensional environment with variable perception-based aspects. His model factors in variability and in fact encourages a generative approach to astral projection and what is perceived there, as opposed to an arrested approach which limits us to only one paradigm of astral reality. With such variability it's still possible to encounter other people on the astral plane. Sometimes this occurs when the projector focuses on finding a specific person, and occasionally it occurs by accident. Also the medium of guided journeys allows purposeful interaction with people projecting into the "same" environment. Subjective realities bleed into each other forming a collage of beliefs and concepts. The various paradigms and beliefs create in the astral plane various realities that are real for the people who experience and accept them as real. If we allow ourselves to be limited by what others tell us the astral plane is, we choose to accept their subjective realities over our own. But as always a magician can consciously choose to change what is experienced. In the end the astral plane isn't so much about reality as it's about endless possibilities to explore and work with. It's up to each of us to determine just what is useful to believe in when we project.

Only in challenging the limitations of the past can we move forward into the future and keep magic at the forefront of innovation and creativity within not only magical practice, but society in general. The work of the past can be relied upon as a reference, but to solely repeat what others have done is to become trapped in their ideas and concepts. Draw on prior work where it's useful, but critically question it and your acceptance of it as well. Apply this to the astral realm and ask yourself this: What is YOUR model of the astral realm?

The astral plane allows us to connect with the imagination and work with it in a much more direct way than we just happen to day dream or fantasize about doing something. One might wonder if the astral plane is really just an access point to the imagination if it's all that useful. I think it is useful because it allows us to integrate our imagination into our magical work. Indeed, the imagination is one of the most powerful tools we have because it allows us to conceptualize possibilities. The astral planes can be thought of as a staging area, where you initially work with possibilities to turn them into reality. However there's also a downside with the astral plane.

Fan Culture and the Astral Planes

Even as we need to challenge and experiment, we also need to recognize the potential shortcomings that occur with working on the astral plane. A while back I read an account where a woman believed she was married to Sephiroth from *Final Fantasy Seven*. Another person claimed she was married to Severus Snape from the *Harry Potter* universe. In both cases the marriages occurred on the astral plane or through dreams. The people involved didn't have a relationship with another person in everyday life. These aren't the only cases either. There are other cases where people have "married" pop culture characters. In almost each of these cases its characters that exhibit negative behaviors and actions, and seem to feed off of the obsessiveness of the fans. Are these marriages real? Perhaps, perhaps not.

As I'll show further down there is a case to be made for having a healthy astral marriage with a pop culture (or other) entity, but in some situations, it's a case of taking an interest to the extreme, to the point that it becomes unhealthy for everyone involved. In such cases the entities seem to insist on one relationship dynamic over others and the actual person involved with said entity is obsessed to a point that little else seems to matter to them, including maintaining relationships (romantic/sexual, or otherwise) with other people in their life. The pop culture entity that the person's obsessed with is fed power by the belief and devotion of the person. And that's the real danger of this fixation, because when a person fixates on an entity to the point that they thinks it's married to them there's the possibility that the entity is feeding off the person. It's similar to the legend of the succubus or incubus who comes at night and feeds on its lover, while tantalizing the lover with fantasies.

Sephiroth is a good example of this. He's a vampyric entity that wants to destroy the world and become a god. He may not exist physically in our reality, but the belief in him creates enough energy for him to take form on the astral plane. Now add someone in who believes they are married to him and what you get is an entity drawing on that person's life force and at the same time isolating them from the people who could probably help them. If it seems far-fetched, just consider that some fan forums are obsessive enough about how their favorite characters are treated that they form cults (as is evident by several different LiveJournal communities devoted to the literal worship of Sephiroth). In other cases, some fans actually claim that they have become the character or have bonded with the character to the point that the character has an active presence in their lives. These fans treat a character such as Sephiroth as an active entity that is also part of their existence, to the point that they sometimes let him encompass their existence. As someone who's invoked pop culture entities, I find it very important to recognize that while it can be a very fulfilling relationship to work with such an entity, it's also important to not let yourself obsess over it. Moderation is key in magic…otherwise you can end up fairly delusional.

Fans are rather unique because their interests in particular stories or characters can sometimes provide enough energy to make what they focus on come to life. It allows fans to find other people who are part of their subculture and the social experience can even include very spiritual and magic intensive experiences, but it can also lead to such occurrences as the examples mentioned above.

While pop culture can be used as a medium for magical practice, there is the danger of buying into it too much, and this danger is most apparent on the astral plane. The astral plane is a subjective reality, which means that it can take what's in your imagination and give it form, especially if you don't have the training needed to control your thought processes. When creating your own model of the astral realm, or for that matter interacting with an entity there, you have to question whether it's a wishful fantasy or reality or a mixture of the two. The way this can really be tested is found in the effects that such interactions have on the physical plane and I'm not talking about finding love hickies on you after a particularly hot and sweaty astral journey with Sephiroth.

Still, while it's evident that some of these relationships can be dangerous, it's also true that others can be healthy, particularly when balanced with relationships with other people and interests in other hobbies, spiritualities, and life in general. The key is to not get obsessed to the point that only the entity matters. A precedent for this can be found in Voodoo. Sometimes the Lwa will demand that a person marry one of them. That person could already be married to a person, but may still have to also marry the Lwa (and sometimes not just one, but at least several in order to provide balance to the relationships). Additionally, there are definite benefits for both/all participants, rather than the Lwa being a parasite in the life of the human being. When such a marriage occurs, the person has specific days on which they are devoted to the Lwa alone, but s/he is not expected to give their entire life to the

Lwa-marriage. While it's not the only religion where marriage to a god or other entity occurs, it's the best-known to Western occultism. This approach can be applied to a pop culture entity.

Let me provide an example of what a healthy astral marriage with an entity can entail. I've worked with the character of Thiede or Aghama quite a lot in the Deharan system of magic created by Storm Constantine. One of the workings I frequently did to contact him is called the gateway ritual. The practitioner astral projects into the astral plane and then rides a spirit beast or Sedim to a palace. In the palace there is a series of mirrors, which act as gateways into the Wraeththu universe. I would usually project myself into that universe and "ride" the body of a Wraeththu so I could interact with Theide.

My workings with this particular god form were focused on an astral marriage with the goal being to create another entity from the union. Over the course of several months I met with Thiede and had what might be considered astral sex, but with the purpose of impregnating the Wraeththu I rode with a pearl or baby. Once this was achieved, my astral workings changed, focusing more on the pregnancy process and eventual birth and hatching of the pearl into a new Dehar, Kiraziel, who became the Dehar of wishes. At this point I began to work with Kiraziel and prepared him for another working I had in mind, which he would help me fulfill. I was and am still married to Thiede to this day and still set aside time which is specifically for him, but at that time the work with Kiraziel took over a lot of my focus, as is often the case with children.

At this point, you may wonder if I'm deluded. However, you will know something is really occurring in the astral when there is a resonance that occurs in the physical realm. As an example, my workings with Thiede were also driven toward learning more about space/time magic and from him I learned the DNA meditation technique (as detailed in *Space/Time Magic*) that I and others have used with good results. This technique was grounded in the physical world when probabilities evoked via it manifested in the physical realm. Likewise my workings with first Thiede and then Kiraziel would also produce resonance (with them) and manifestation of several desired results into my life.

I created Kiraziel with the specific purpose of granting a wish in my life, in this case to find a magical partner. This occurred on the winter solstice of 2003. Shortly after I created him, I met someone who I thought might be my magical partner, but was not. At first I wondered if I had deluded myself, if the astral projection work had just been a fantasy. But then I considered as well that finding such a partner would not occur on my schedule, but would occur in a time and place that was right for finding the person. In the summer of 2005 I met someone, who became my magical partner (at the time). About eight weeks into the relationship, Kiraziel visited me and indicated this was the person I'd been looking for and that he considered the wish fulfilled. It was now up to me to follow through on what I wished for.

Granted it was almost two years before this wish came true, but when I consider the time span of the ritual to create

Kiraziel, it took approximately just under two months for the working to occur. I think that the time spans correlated with each other, in the sense that one month of ritual work could represent one year in a person's life. Kiraziel knew that it would take time and effort to find my magical partner. However what really told me that Kiraziel had manifested in my life was a death-rebirth ritual I did shortly after he'd been created. This ritual was focused on inducing a state of near death for several days and then bringing me back to life on the third day. Kiraziel played a role as one of the rebirthers. When the final stage of the working was completed, a witness to it felt his presence very strongly and asked who he was. I explained my previous ritual (which she didn't know about).

It should be borne in mind that I told Kiraziel that I wanted him to find me a magical partner who fit what I was looking for, no matter how long it took. I didn't do other specific rituals afterwards for this purpose, beyond being guided one night in January 2005 to make a collage. Even though that collage was random and unfocused it ironically (or magically) ended up having an unattributed photograph of my magical partner that was printed in a pagan newspaper in it (before I ever met her), as well attributes central to what I was looking for. The guidance I felt was an inspired guidance, a voice that said to make a collage and see what would happen. I made the collage to foretell events in my immediate future, but now I suspect that Kiraziel was working through me to use the collage to help with his search.

Although astral projection can be a useful skill to learn and work with you need to keep yourself grounded and focused on living in this reality. An astral marriage is fine and well, if the purpose is to do more than try to live your dream boat fantasies with the entity in question. In Voodoo, as well as in my example, there are some expectations of devotion and focus, but there is also an understanding that the entity doesn't overshadow the life of the person.

It's easy to get caught up in the feeling of being loved by such an entity, but if it doesn't exist in the physical realm and is keeping you focused on itself, chances are it's using you as a source of energy. Certainly Sephiroth would have no problem using a person foolish enough to be in love with him as a sort of battery. And as such you should be doubly careful with who or what you choose to work with on the astral plane, because not only are you giving form and life to such a being, you are also inviting it to that place, where it has some power. If that occurs such a being could easily create problems for you. I recommend banishing in the astral plane using your preferred technique (and if you don't have one yet then you probably shouldn't be doing this sort of work!) and then banishing in the physical world, followed up by getting rid of any paraphernalia associated with the entity. For someone in love with Sephiroth this would mean getting rid of any *Final Fantasy* material associated with him. If that seems extreme, just remember that an entity can and will use any vector that allows it to have a connection with you. By getting rid of the physical objects you cut off the connection.

A better route though is to work with such entity in moderation. I don't work with either Thiede or Kiraziel often. My workings with them are occasional, done with respect, but with an awareness that I also need to attend to matters in this world. By moderating the time I spend working with them I can get what I need from my workings and maintain those relationships, but without compromising my life in other ways. Remember to test these workings as well. Look for physical manifestations of the work and make sure it's goal oriented, as opposed to supporting a non-existent love life that becomes the entity's cash cow. Finally, keep your emotions on a tight rein. Work with the entity, but keep yourself grounded on what you need to accomplish in your everyday life. Remember that the astral plane you work with is your model of that reality and as such can be changed if you so choose. But also remember that because the astral plane is your model of that reality it can become such an ideal model that it sabotages your purpose. Who wouldn't want to live in an ideal world where everything goes right? On the surface, such a reality in the astral plane might seem ideal, but carefully consider that it could also be a delusion fashioned by your desires, but one that doesn't help you meet those desires. Want someone in your life? Sephiroth might seem like the perfect boyfriend on the astral plane, but it's not like you can introduce him to your friends or family or do any of the other fun things you can do with a person on the physical plane. Whatever astral marriages you have are in the end a combination of the product of your mind and your consciousness interacting with other consciousnesses. Recognize that and you will recognize whether what you are doing is a delusion or a means to an end that can help you manifest what you really need in your life.

Astral Temples

The final thought I have is that the astral plane, and whatever model it is for you, is one that's useful for mapping out your consciousness. An astral temple is an excellent example of this principle. The temple is created on the astral plane by the practitioner. It's a home away from home. You shape the environment with your thoughts, creating a building, which becomes your temple. You also place whatever you feel belongs in that temple. It can have as many rooms as you need it to have, and whatever symbols, statues, or whatever else you feel belongs in the temple. When you form an astral temple, you might want to ask yourself why you chose some of the symbols and other materials in the temple and if any of it correlates to your perceptions of everyday reality. While the astral temple is primarily used to do magical workings, it's also a gateway to your subconscious. You could even fashion doorways in the temple and use them to access parts of your consciousness that you normally wouldn't interact with. That particular kind of working is useful for meeting with aspects of yourself that you want to integrate into your core personality.

What might even be more useful is using the doorways to access a problematic situation. You may wish to work with someone else and do an astral pathworking. In such a case you would astral project, and have the person read from a script that would help you create a relatively neutral astral reality you could work with. They would guide you through a scenario that would allow you to address the problem in a manner that resolved it. I've used pathworking techniques to help me overcome subconscious triggers and issues and permanently change the behaviors in a manner that's beneficial. There are other ways to accomplish those goals (as I've covered in *Inner Alchemy*), but this technique is one you can use in the astral plane and a way of healthily exploring its potentials. The person that's with you can always bring you back and ground you afterwards.

The astral plane is what you make of it. Rely on no one model too much, but don't dismiss them either. Even the seven plane dualistic model has its uses, but what really matters is that you recognize that the astral plane is in large part comprised of your subjective experience of it and so while it's useful, it can also be misleading.

Exercise:

What have your experiences with the astral plane been? Do you agree or disagree with my analysis of the astral plane. Why?

Lesson 22: Banishing, Shielding, and the Process of Magic

There's a lot that has been said about banishing, so much so that some magicians who (R.J. Stewart and Jason Miller amongst others) argue that Western Magic is obsessed with banishing in a way that can be unhealthy. I find myself in agreement with them regarding the act of banishment, and in a way I see this obsession with banishment as an example of how our mainstream culture's obsession with cleanliness has extended even to magical work. Not that I have anything against being clean or living in a clean environment, but it is worth noting that how banishment is approached is similar to what I mentioned about divination. It's used to the point of overkill, and when banishment is used to that degree it indicates a lack of understanding about both banishment and magical work in general.

The reason I make that rather controversial statement is simple. If you do banishment after a magical working you are clearing out your space, but perhaps you are also clearing out the connection between yourself and the magical working. This suggests that at the very least banishment needs to be more targeted in its focus, specifically what you are banishing and what you aren't banishing. I like R. J. Stewart's approach to banishment (See Sphere of Art 1 for more information), because the focus is on doing the banishment before the actual magical working, with the understanding that what you are banishing is the influences, energies, entities, etc. that could interfere with the working, but that you aren't banishing the magical working in and of itself.

To my mind, that is the correct way to approach banishing. You want to clear out what doesn't belong in order to open yourself fully to what you want to work with. And you don't want to banish what you worked with afterwards, because there needs to be a connection between yourself and the magical work that lasts beyond the ritual. The whole point of doing the magical work is that you are transforming reality by manifesting a specific possibility into it. I find the best way to keep that connection strong is to embody the possibility. In other words when you do the magical work, you bring the possibility into your life by melding it to your physical body. You embody the magic and the possibility you want to manifest into reality. That embodiment directs the expression of the possibility into reality through your actions, and acceptance of the place that the possibility moves you to. Below is an article I wrote about banishing, which I've included here for this lesson that illustrates the concepts I mentioned above:

Banishment through detachment

When the concept of banishing is considered within magic, it's used to indicate a cleansing and/or clearing out of space. This can involve physical objects, but also includes spiritual energies that may have been worked with, but are not part and parcel of you and your environment.

This traditional approach does work for some people. When I banish, before and after working magic, I sometimes visualize the energy being cleaned away and will even do some of the things mentioned above. Even the act of cleaning the house is an act of banishment and purification. Other people I know will use the common neopagan technique of sweeping the ritual area with an actual broom to get rid of both physical and energetic dust. Unwanted energy is removed in the act of cleaning, while ideally the desired energy is emphasized.

However, there are times when a different approach to banishment is needed. Sure, you can take the phone off the ringer and physically clean your space, but what if you have some current magical workings in the room you're doing the banishing in? What if you work with an entity and that entity is housed in an object in the room you work magic in? And finally what if you just want to challenge your discipline? There is another way to do banishing…if you're willing to learn detachment.

I have on the walls of my home sigil paintings I've created. These sigil paintings are always being charged and fired by the attention given to them by the residents and visitors. Traditionally sigils are gotten rid of soon after they are created. The energy of the sigil is banished by way of destroying it. At the same time the act of banishing is also the means of getting the energy to work, to manifest the desire. However, I find that sigil workings are intensified, not through a destruction of the sigil, but through the retaining of it and the keeping of it in a place where I see it every day.

Although some would argue that by seeing the sigil every day I'm preventing the manifestation of the desire, I find that after a couple days I have forgotten the purpose of the sigil. The physical shell of the sigil becomes part of the background and also part of my subconscious. I banish the sigil by detaching myself from the physical reminder of it; it no longer has meaning despite the fact that it continues to exist in a material form. I find that this kind of practice is good for discipline purposes, because if you can learn to block out what is around you and make it meaningless you can work magic under circumstances where you might otherwise easily be distracted and not have the benefit of doing a traditional banishing.

The principle of detachment works through finding no meaning in what's around you. If nothing has meaning to you, then it has no power to affect you. You (temporarily) detach yourself from the meanings you invest in the physical objects you own, the relationships you have with other people, and in the magical projects you're involved in. Any of these factors could distract you from focusing your mind in order to achieve your goal. When you banish through detachment, the distractions might still exist, but you ignore them through a focused application of the mind, where everything around you ceases to have meaning. This is an effective way of disciplining yourself when doing magic and also realizing that meaning is a constructed reality as opposed to an inherent reality.

I also approach banishing through the concept of zeroing. This discipline of banishing involves a high level of discipline. To become something you first have to choose not to become something else, which means that you have to banish from yourself every other possible thing you could be, so you can focus on the matter at hand. You don't necessarily have to use the traditional approach of banishing to do that. For example, you might not have the time to physically clear everything out. Instead you must focus on what you wish to work with and block out everything else, making it part of the background, as opposed to being relevant to your reality. Although everything else is in the background it doesn't exist for you. Your focus is on is the magical act instead.

To develop this ability to detach ourselves, we want to do an exercise with our senses. Because it's our senses that bring us stimuli and information, we must first learn to quiet them, so we can focus our energy elsewhere. It's best to do this exercise in a highly distracting setting. If you can banish all the distractions in such a setting then your home or wherever you work magic will be a breeze in comparison. And believe it or not, you probably have done this kind of banishment before; you just may not have realized it. If you've ever found yourself really engaged by a T.V. program you watched, or a book you read, to the point that nothing else seemed to matter, you've banished all other reality except for what you were engaged in.

I recommend some place outdoors where there's a lot of activity, such as a plaza in a city or a mall. Regardless of where you go, what you want to do is focus on one of the five senses, blocking the other senses out. For instance, touch everything around you and really feel the texture; ignore everything you see, hear, smell, and taste (other than what you need to avoid, say, walking into a tree). The idea is to learn how to focus your attention on one specific sensation, while detaching yourself from the rest. If you get distracted, start over. If you feel self-conscious about doing this activity, remember that detaching yourself doesn't just include physical sensations, but also emotion. Examine why you feel self-conscious and then detach yourself from that feeling.

Another way to do this exercise is to pick an object and look at it as intently as possible. Begin writing about that object, describing it in as much detail as you can. Again the key is to focus to the point where nothing meaningful exists but that object. If something distracts you, bring your attention back to the object and start over. By learning to focus like this, you discipline your mind and at the same time banish what is around you by choosing not to regard it as meaningful.

Starting this exercise with some physical stresses can help you achieve an awareness of how your body can distract you through sensation. The key to taming the mind is found through taming the body. Once you've mastered focusing on a physical level, apply the detachment principle to the mental level. Detach yourself from the physical sensations you are feeling and focus on a concept you desire to bring into reality. Visualize the concept in concrete terms. How will this concept manifest into reality? How do you fit into this concept? Ignore any stray thoughts, focusing only on becoming the concept you wish to manifest. Everything else does not exist. All that does exist in this moment of manifestation is you and the concept you seek to bring forth.

This exercise is somewhat similar to some of Bardon's work where he has the magician focus on projecting themselves into an object. The goal is to shift the consciousness into the object and experience reality through its filter while detaching yourself from the awareness of your body (Bardon 2001a). Bardon's exercises are excellent supplementary material to the exercises mentioned here because they show the magician how to control their consciousness, one of the hardest tasks of magic and also one of the most important.

Another thing to remember about detaching yourself is that it does require discipline. I favor discipline in my approaches to magic, because learning how to focus and concentrate under any circumstance allows me to be on top of any situation I'm in. Discipline is essential for organizing how you approach life and deal with situations. A lack of discipline will defeat you every time, whereas having it will help you concentrate on what is and isn't important to each situation you're in. By learning how to detach myself from what is distracting me, I can negate any power the distraction has on me, and in fact take that power and add it to the focused manifestation desired. Once the meaning is taken from something, I also channel its energy into whatever is currently relevant to my efforts.

Sometimes you may find that the traditional approach to banishing won't work because of the environment. For instance, how do you banish a pesky co-worker? I've found that by learning to detach myself, learning to no longer put meaning into the co-worker, that the situation changes. The co-worker is banished, becoming part of the scenery, and I'm free to focus on more important matters.

Continued work with detachment doesn't lead to less of an interest in what's occurring around you. The most important thing to remember about this type of banishing is that you determine the meaning of everything in your life. It's up to you to decide the degree of importance that a person, object, event, etc. has in your life. Just remember not to get stuck in a detached perspective. It can be easy to stay detached, because you're focused so much on a particular goal. When I'm focused on magic, nothing else matters, but once I'm done with the magical act I re-invest meaning in what matters to me, the people in my life and what I enjoy doing when I'm not practicing magic. I imagine color coming back into everything around me, which in turn brings back the meanings I associate with everything.

The goal of banishing is not merely to remove distracting influences, but also to help center you so that your efforts can be directed toward what you seek. Clear out the distractions from your life and you will find that you can accomplish anything and meet any problem head on in a successful manner.

Some further Thoughts on Banishment

I still use detachment as one means of banishing unneeded energies, but over the years since I wrote that article I've also come across some other techniques. I already mentioned R.J. Stewart's work, and although his book is written in the context of a specific tradition, you could easily pick it up and work with the concept, and personalize it to your own work. In fact, that's what I did when I read the Sphere of Art and experimented with the technique. I liked what he wrote, but I thought it best to personalize the sphere of art technique in my own way. Instead of drawing on the archangels to seal the sphere of art, I chose to work with my own entities: Elephant, Thiede, Purson, and the Spider Queen of Time. Beyond that everything I did was essentially the same, but my point is that even a "tradition specific" banishing (or any other type of working) can be modified and adapted to fit your own personal cosmology and still be effective. The underlying principles and how the technique work doesn't change just because you change the window dressings.

Another technique that I think of as banishing is one I learned from Antero Alli's work with Paratheatre as expressed in his book: "Towards an Archaeology of the Soul" Antero's approach to banishing involved assuming a state of no-form, essentially clearing out your emotions, thoughts etc, and at the same time relaxing the physical awareness of your body so that your posture, face etc is a blank slate. Banishing all of that allows you to then choose what you want to embody in the space around you and within you. The benefit of this approach to banishing is that much like the sphere of art and the detachment technique it involves first taking out what you don't need and then putting into the space what you do need. In a sense what banishment really is, is a technique for not only clearing space, but also building space. And when we understand banishment from this perspective we are better able to apply it in a way that makes our magical works more effective.

Some Thoughts on Shielding

Shielding is sometimes associated with banishing. There are different schools of thought about shielding. Some people think it's necessary to shield, and other people feel that shielding blocks them from effectively working with magic. I'm of the opinion that it's worthwhile to know how to shield and that if you are doing it right, you shouldn't have any difficulties with the shielding blocking your effectiveness in magic.

A while back my wife was on a spiritual retreat and she told me many of the people attending were visited by ghosts and had weird dreams. She was one of the few who didn't because she shielded her room. I had to admit I was puzzled that any occultist wouldn't know how to or wouldn't think to shield themselves, but I've found that there are occultists who won't shield themselves because they think they'll miss something if they do (like a night of bad sleep) or because shields will make their magical work less effective.

Personally I'm not willing to go anywhere without having shielded myself and when I sleep in a hotel or anywhere else, I always have the space I sleep in warded. And I think what amazes me the most is that many of these occultists don't seem to know how to do even a basic shielding. I know there are books on the topic, so I'm not sure why they don't know, but it's odd and it speaks to a fundamental lack of training. However, I've also realized that they might have the training but still choose not to shield themselves because of a perceived disadvantage of shielding themselves.

When I first started practicing magic, one of the first activities I learned and performed daily was shielding. There were a couple techniques provided in Ted Andrew's books on working with spirits...They had you create a shield by vocalizing the names of gods and visualizing different energies enfolding your physical and spiritual surroundings with protective energy. I noticed that when I did that practice that I did feel a sense of protection, as well as a clearing of the space around me, so I did it every day. I don't do that particular practice anymore, but I still do shielding each day, for the benefit of shielding, but also for the benefit it provides me in terms of starting my day. I feel good, and I feel focused. It takes me a half hour each day to do the practice, and its well worth the time. I consider shielding to be part of my meditation practice.

Any person who chooses to practice magic knows that they are inviting a different awareness of the universe that brings with it possible encounters and experiences that can nonetheless be filtered out through shields. I shield so that I can focus on manifesting the experiences that truly speak to the core of my practice as a spiritual and practical application of my experience of the world. I don't leave myself open to experience everything, but instead filter the experience to focus on enhancing what I really want to bring into my life.

Some people have argued that creating and maintaining a shield takes up energy and that this makes your other magical work less effective because of the energy you are having to put into maintaining those shields. One suggested way for getting around that issue is to create entities who specifically are tasked to create shields and maintain them while you do your work.

I have my own work around when it comes to shields. One of the techniques I used which has been discussed above in banishing is a Zeroing technique that William Gray writes about in Magical Ritual Methods. The zeroing technique involves creating a space of Zero Time, Zero Space, and Zero Event, essentially a space/time where nothing exists save the practitioner AND what the practitioner chooses to bring into that space/time. I use this technique with my magical work in general and it can, for all intents and purposes be considered a "shielding" technique.

Now when this technique is used it does serve to create a very specific space/time that excludes anything not brought into it by the practitioner. However the beauty of it is that you can bring into it exactly what you need to work with, be it an entity, possibility or something else. Additionally, what is also significant is that when you wrap up the magical working, and return that space/time to regular space/time, you merge it with and embody it into reality, making a seamless transition where there is no resistance to the possibility being manifested. That problem of not connecting to the world or being able to effect material events isn't a problem with this technique. You draw in the event you want to affect, as well as the possibility you want to use to solve the problem, work the magic and mesh it into your own identity, and then release the zeroing space/time, or sphere of art and allow yourself and the magic to fully reintegrate into the world around you, embodying a new reality in the process.

Back when I did shielding in other ways, I also had my shields set up so that I didn't have to maintain them. I let the influences, people, etc. that were trying to interfere do the maintaining for me. It always worked like a charm and can be used with wards as well, when shielding a place. The shields only activate when something directs energy that would be harmful or distracting to the magician. And those shields are fed by the very energy, influence, etc. being directed against them. Simple, effective, no draining of your energy required.

If you know what you're doing, a given act such as shielding shouldn't have any of the problems such as not being able to effect the material world or being a drain on your energy. Defining a technique by its limitations means you accept those limitations and don't question them. While you should know what the limitations of a given technique are, define it in terms of what it could do and then experiment! Don't settle for explanations offered by others about the limitations and problems of a given technique. There's always a way to solve the problem or limitation of a given technique if you are willing to experiment. I only encountered those problems when I first started practicing magic and when I encountered them, I got curious and decided to see what I could to fine tune my shields and avoid the issues they mentioned in the comments. It took a bit of a work, but it's nothing that anyone couldn't discover, provided they are curious enough and willing to experiment with a given technique. Why settle for allowing a technique to limit you? My answer: Don't settle…experiment.

Lesson 23: The Process of Magic and Attunement

When I talk about attunement, I'm not talking about some new age concept where you are trying to attune yourself the harmonies of the universe. Attunement, as a magical activity, is a process of connection and identification with the natural elements of the environment. It's not the same as doing an invocation or evocation of an entity, because the focus isn't on working with an entity per se. The focus is on connecting with the land and the elements or with other primal forces that you can connect with. This can be a powerful way to connect yourself with natural resources that you can draw on, but be aware you also need to offer something in return.

There's a couple terms I'm going to use that will help us differentiate this technique from evocation and invocation.

Ley Lines - Typically ley lines are depicted as lines of energy that connect places of power (or power spots) to each other. Many people think of ley lines as lines of force that run along the surface of the planet, but this is an inaccurate perspective fostered in part by a humancentric perspective. I think of ley lines as lines of power that are also the spiritual energy of the planet, as well as its connection to the cosmos. A ley line doesn't just run on the surface of the Earth, but also to the core of the Earth and there are also ley lines that connect to the other planets and the sun. At the same time, I think it's also possible to create artificial leylines. Highways are examples of artificial leylines, but you could think of a computer network as having multiple leylines as well. Leylines then can be thought of as more than just some nebulous energy or life force. Ley lines are information, albeit rarified forms of information. The information you get from a natural ley line will differ from the information you'd get from an artificial ley line.

Power Spots - Power spots or places of power are concentrated areas of energy, or if you will a confluence of elemental/planetary energies. Power spots can also be artificial, such as a city, or other examples I'll draw on below. Power spots provide magicians access to energy that can be tapped or used, but some care needs to be taken with it, because a power spot isn't just a confluence of energy, but also has some level of consciousness. I think of power spots as similar to egregores, but different because they are elemental in nature. Ley lines originate from and travel to power spots.

The technique of attunement is based on the principle of connection, but it ultimately involves forming a connection of knowing. What I mean by that is to really connect with a ley line or power spot, you need to experience it on a very intimate level, know it in such a way that it becomes part of your identity. This means there's some level of research involved in really connecting to a power spot or to the ley lines. Let me give you a couple of personal examples.

Raymire's Hollow

When I lived in York, PA, there was a place called Raymire's Hollow where according to local legend a folk magician had lived. Not only had he lived there, but he also practiced magic there, particularly hexcraft. It was also said that he cursed a rival and that rival, in desperation, visited him and murdered him. The rival even burned Raymire's house, but swore that even he'd killed Raymire, that he could see him coming after him. It's a colorful legend, based on actual events. If you ever drive out to Raymire's Hollow you'll feel a difference in the land. It feels darker, even at the height of noon and no one will live in or near the hollow. They feel too uncomfortable with the energy. It's a power spot marked by the events that occurred and also by the Spirit of Raymire.

When I was eighteen I visited Raymire's Hollow. Everything said about it was true. When you drove in you felt this supernatural chill. And when you went in at night, it was darker in the hollow, then anywhere around it, and you could feel the energy of the land and also Raymire's restless spirit. I chose to bond myself to that power spot, because I wanted to see what would happen. I walked the land, communing with it. I walked in the remains of Raymire's house and communed with him. I drew a knife and cut myself and made an offering of blood to the land, partially as a way to connect with the Hollow as a power spot and also partially as an offering the element of Earth. I felt myself connect with the land, with the power spot, and with Raymire, felt myself extend into the awareness of the area. After that day I could connect with the energy of that place at will and draw on it. I can even do it this day, living in Portland, Oregon, because that power spot is something I connected to. I created a connection that goes deeper than any physical distance and I've never chosen to severe that connection (although you can do that too).

Kent State

When I lived in Kent Ohio, while trying for a PH.D, one of the first activities I did involved connecting with land, and more particularly with the land of Kent State University. Much as with Raymire's Hollow, I walked the land, and got to know it very intimately. Instead of offering blood, I choose to create spit sigils which would be activated by the sun and would bond my energy with the energy of the land, although I got a bit more than I realized. I connected with the land, but I also connected with the Genius of Kent State. I realized in retrospect that attuning to a power spot at a university would connect me with more than just the confluence of natural energies. It'd also connect me with the confluence of human energy, in other words all the activity that students, faculty, etc. were involved in, as well as the simple fact that Kent State university, as a presence was in the thought of pretty much anyone who lived there. The university defined the town and as such was a confluence of energies.

When I left Kent, I severed my connection. It involved walking the land and doing a banishing at each spot I'd done the spit sigils. I knew I needed to sever the connection because I wasn't staying in the area, and because it helped me with emotional closure.

Other Examples of Power Spots

The two examples above showed what happened when I attuned myself to two different types of power spots. One was natural, the other artificial. There was an element of human interaction in each and that is important only in the sense that working with a power spot typically involves a human element. But let's consider a few other types of power spots (Don't worry, we'll get to the ley lines).

For example, what about a city? Having lived in a few cities and visited others I can safely say that cities are their power spots, and fairly powerful ones. A city is a confluence of natural and artificial influences, as well as a genius spirit and each city is distinctive in its own right. Cities even choose the kind of people they want or don't want living in them. Seattle couldn't stand me (and the feeling was mutual). I didn't mesh well with the energy of that city. Portland, on the other hand seemed to fit like a glove, but what's interesting is that the five districts of Portland all have their own distinctive presences. South East Portland feels different from North East Portland, and North Portland is different from both of them. The west side is something else. One could argue that there are power spots within power spots, and it wouldn't be inaccurate.

Cities, as power spots, aren't just defined by the activities of the people. Portland has the Columbia and the Willamette rivers flowing through it, as well as a number of city parks, and a variety of other natural features that also contribute to the creation of a power spot. But the human oriented activities also define it. Landmarks such as the Chinese Gardens or Pittock Mansion contribute to the essence of Portland, as do highways that go through it (though the highways are leylines). The bustle of business, networking events...all of it creates this power spot called Portland.

What about a state or a province? When I moved out to Seattle one thing I and my partner at the time noticed was that each state felt different and seemed to have its own distinctive personality. The landscape of each state signified the personality of the state. New Mexico, although it is right by Arizona, nonetheless seems to have a different landscape, and a different kind of energy. Mind you these were impressions formed while driving through the states, but what's also interesting is that even the people of a given state seem to by some extension represent the personality of the state. It's as if the identity of the state has merged with the identity of the person. What I can also say is that living in Oregon and connecting with it as a state feels different from how Ohio or Pennsylvania felt, and that my experience with the people in Oregon also is different the people in Pennsylvania and Ohio. I could be making more out of this than is there, but it's an intriguing thought.

There are also natural power spots. The Multnomah Falls is a good example of one. The falls attract thousands of visitors and what makes it a power spot is partially that traffic but also the way the natural forces combine. In fact, I'd argue that how one knows one has found a power spot is by the observation of how it draws other people. Power spots want to be found, if only because it is a confluence of energy and that includes the energy people put toward it.

What about Ley Lines?

I haven't forgotten ley lines. I think that the main difference between a ley line and a powerspot is that a leyline involves movement. A leyline may connect with and pass through a power spot, but it never stops at the power spot. A leyline is a current of elemental energy, and like a power spot it can be worked with, both in terms of finding power spots, but also in and of itself. The other important characteristic of a ley line is that ley lines aren't confined to this planet. In other words ley lines connect to other planets and stars. I think of ley lines as spiritual channels that serve to connect everything together. It could even be postulated that ley lines are part of what allows us to connect with planetary energy, elemental energy etc.

Ley lines start at the core of each world. The core is the heart of the planet. The ley lines are the spiritual blood of the planet. To truly connect with a leyline, start with a meditation at the core. Make yourself as comfortable as possible, using whatever technique you use for meditation. Then direct your consciousness to the core of the Earth. I recommend that you connect with it carefully...it's a very powerful force. In fact you may not want to connect with it at all. But what you'll feel or see around it are leylines. Some will be going in, while others will be going out. Connect with one going out and follow it, flow into it and see where it takes you, both on the Earth, but also into space. If you follow a ley line into space eventually it'll connect with a planet, or with the sun and you can interact with the energy from the planet or the sun. I found this useful because it helped me see how ley lines are really a connective between this planet and others. In a sense I felt like I experienced the rhythm of the universe when I did this kind of working.

Exercise:

Find a power spot or a leyline in your area. How did you identify it? What would you do to work with it?

Lesson 24: The Role of Limitation in the Process of Magic

The majority of occult texts don't typically deal with the topic of limitation in magic. I've seen it discussed in Kevin Townley's work on the Cube of Space, and also by R.J. Stewart. Those are the only authors who've discussed limitation as a magical principle. In general it's ignored or people might even say that they thought the whole point of magic was to help them get past limitations. But a considered understanding of limitation as it applies to magic can help us more meaningfully work with it and appreciate it as a principle that informs how we practice. R. J. Stewart says that the principle of limitation limits the amount of force in favor of form. In other words, to create a form, or manifest a physical result, you have to limit the amount of force used. This principle doesn't just apply to magic, but applies to the world around us in general. If you look at how just about anything is made, the force involved in the creation has to be carefully managed. If it isn't then you ruin what you are making.

Limitation has value as a principle precisely because the movement from potential into reality involves the focus of force into the creation of form. Magic isn't about tossing fireballs or levitating. It's about the focus of force to create measurable results or changes within a person's life, but even change is limited to some degree by the physicality in which it is expressed in. When an idea becomes physical, it takes on form, and in that process sheds the potential (the force) it previously had. The manifestation of form is the acceptance of the limitations that form brings. Ironically those same limitations can still provide a lot in the way of freedom. A limitation creates limits, but also creates ways for you to interact with the limits.

In the anime Neon Genesis Evangelion, in one of the final episodes, they illustrate the principle of limitation. If you have boundless freedom or infinite possibility, but no limitation, you can't manifest it. But if you add a defined reality, then you have limitation, and you no longer have infinite possibilities. However that limitation allows you to actually do things (in the case of NGE, the character could walk on the line), whereas infinite possibilities doesn't allow you to do anything, because there is nothing to limit it. The realm of ideas is also the realm of endless possibilities or chaos. Nothing is true and everything is permitted, but without limitation all that exists is endless potential. The change from possibility to reality involves some form of limitation. This is why a magical working is really a descriptor and definer of the possibility being brought into reality. In other words, a magical working in and of itself limits the expression of possibility into specific results. The benefit of this is that you achieve a specific result that can be applied to your life, other people's lives etc. The more improbable your possibility, the harder it is to bring into reality, for the simple fact is that it requires more "energy" to overcome the distinct limitations that we deal with on a practical level. At a certain point the exertion of so much "energy" becomes more and more impractical.

Limitation, in and of itself, is a form of force, in the sense that the limits we encounter actually serve to create possibilities that we can interact with. Sheer potential, which has no limitation, can't really be worked with, until some form of limitation is imposed on it. A blank sheet of paper is raw potential, but once you draw a line, you've limited the potential and started to create the form. The limitation of potential still creates possibilities, but those possibilities are defined by the limitation, and have a relationship with it. The exploration of that relationship is what allows a magician to discover possibilities and begin to move them from potential into reality via magic.

Limitation provides an awareness of boundaries, but also provides the magician something to strive for, in terms of bending the rules. While force must be limited in order to manifest form, drawing on force is necessary to create form. Potential doesn't become reality unless force is applied to potential. The realization of form, or the result, is due to the application of force to potential, shaping it, defining it, limiting it, and thus creating form. Force is needed to create form, but the application of force necessarily is a fixation on a specific form or result. Nonetheless bending the rules around how much force can be applied as well what modifications can be made to a form is something the experimental magician is willing to do. As an example, when I first started working with elemental energies, I offered my blood for the essence of the elementals. I bent the rules a bit, in terms of how I could work with the elemental energies, which allows me to work with them more closely. I think the subsequent evolution of elemental work I've done is a benefit of bending the rules around how much force can be worked with. I have found some other ways to bend the rules on limitation, particularly with evocation.

My approach to evocation, whether it's evoking an entity or a specific type of energy, involves the use of a painting or drawing as a gateway. The act of creating the drawing or painting is the initial evocation of the entity, usually finalized with a consecration of some sort. The purpose of it is to create a permanent evocation that can be accessed at any time. Instead of having to do another ritual all over again, I prefer to simplify the process, and bend the rules of limitation, which would suggest that a permanent evocation isn't possible because of the amount of energy involved.

Once the drawing or painting is created, the evocation portal is also created. Nothing else needs to be done, save to make sure you close it when not evoking the entity or energy in question. The entire point of it is to remove a lot of effort out of the equation, by making it simple to access to the entity or energy in question when needed, whether in a strict evocation, or to enhance a magical working being done at the time. But it occurs to me that this is also a way around limitation, as R. J. Stewart discussed it. Specifically if the spirits you work with are going to limit how much you can draw on, why not instead create a way to tap into the power current when you need it, where you have a consistent flow of energy or access to enhance or power up your magical workings? You won't necessarily move beyond the limitations imposed, but instead of having to do a lot of work each time, cut down on the effort involved and get the same return you'd have gotten before. It seems like a short cut, but my reason for creating such an approach to evocation was to make it easy to access whatever it was I wanted to work with. I figure if such an entity is willing to work with me, I have its blessing to make that process easier for both of us. So what happens is that the painting/drawing acts as an evocation portal, and actually draws on the native energy of the entity's plane of existence to open itself. If the principle of limitation says that the amount of force needs to be limited to create form, my approach is to use the form to define the amount of force needed to continue to fuel the form and allow it to perform its function. This neatly allows us to get around the limitation and actually use it in our favor to provide a continual access to entity, power, energy, etc. that is evoked.

This also depends on whether or not you accept that such limitations occur when you evoke or invoke an entity. Personally I'm inclined to believe in those limitations as my own experiences suggest just that. For example invoking an entity to do a full on possession of the body takes up a lot of energy, and not just for myself but also the entity. At a certain point there is a strain for the entity as well because it is placing itself in a foreign environment that it's not necessarily suited to. An evocation portal provides a different level of interaction and one that's not as demanding on either side of the equation. The limitation may still be there, but it'll take longer to come up against, which can be useful for prolonged magical workings. It comes down to being aware of a limitation and the figuring out how to bend it, to make it work for you, instead of against you. Limitations are obstructions, so much as guides for what we can or can't do, but the true value of the limitation is that it teaches us how to adapt to it, and grow beyond it. This is true not only in magic, but also in life.

It's worthwhile to consider that limitations aren't set in stone either. While there are always limitations, it's also possible to move those limitations. We move or change our limitations through consistent practice and discipline, as well as through the willingness to experiment and do something beyond the conventional. It is the discovery of the unknown and the willingness to test the known with it that allows us to change limitations. Thus it is important to remember that limitations should only be accepted until you can challenge them. Once you challenge them, you will find that they change. You can handle what they limited you against, and still be able to produce form that manifests the desired reality you've been looking for.

Form is the ultimate expression of limitation. Once form is realized, limitations are a bit more set in stone, as it were. But as I said above the realization of form brings with it, its own liberties and choices that might not otherwise be experienced. Form is a requisite for experience. A possibility is not an experience until it is given form, which is the expression of the possibility on reality. What I mention above about testing limitations still applies in the sense that while a form may have limitations, those can be tinkered with and experimented on. *Inner Alchemy* focuses on some of my experiments with the body, in terms of the overall force it could handle. Thus it is worth considering that one of our main limitations has more to do with how we perceive ourselves to be limited. If we explore form with open curiosity and a willingness to experiment, what we discover is that limits are not as set as perceived. The truth to challenging limitations is that first you challenge the perception of those limitations. Once you have challenged those perceptions, then you begin to discover the reality of the limitations, and you test that reality (such as it may be) and discover to what extent you are truly limited, as well as what you can do within those limits, and using those limits. Magic is one such process for testing limitations, and the point of this lesson is to consider not only where limitations apply to the process of magic, but also where we can modify those limitations. The principle of limitation is an invitation to experiment and test our experiences. We cannot truly know magic until we have tested ourselves in our practice of it, and used that experience to change our awareness of the potential of our forms, and that of the possibilities we manifest. Our next lesson is concerned with the divine union of force and form to create change...to create transformation.

Exercise

How does the principle of limitation apply to your magical work? How have you challenged your perception of limitation and what has it taught you?

Lesson 25: The Process of Magic and Transformation

When I wrote this lesson, I have to admit that Transformation was a recent addition to my process of magic (at the time of original writing 2012). It's not something I thought about until I started reading R. J. Stewart's work and began to apply his ideas about transformation to the work I'd done with Magical Identity. I include this in the process of magic as a way to consider transformation as an integral part of the process.

In Magical Identity, I discussed at length the importance of internal work to the magical process, and to creating an empowered identity for the magician. I also noted that at least in Western Magic there seemed to be a tendency to gloss over the internal work in favor of achieving practical results. Or on the opposite end, the focus would be on a model such as the Tree of Life, but with little focus on doing internal work.

Magic becomes truly effective when you understand that it fundamentally involves change through intentional transformation, and when you also realize that the most effective magic works by changing the internal reality of the magician first, and then changing the environment around him/her. Results based magic that doesn't factor in the needed internal work is typically reactive magic, done more as a reaction to a problem and as an attempt to solve said problem. Results obtained through a reactive approach to magic don't last long. The magician will sabotage themselves because some part of his/her internal reality doesn't agree with the obtained result. While results are important for your process of magic, in terms of tracking the effectiveness of your magical work, they are also important in terms of providing clues for you, in what you need to work on with yourself.

To truly understand transformation and change, you must be willing to shape yourself as well as shape the environment around you. It might even be argued that you need to be willing to be shaped by the magic, in order to truly benefit from it. Fundamentally what is being asked is: "Are you truly ready and willing to handle the responsibility of changing your reality?" You can only answer yes when you've done the internal work that allows you to critically examine your place in the universe and willingly change that place by changing your internal reality. Place, or space isn't just a physical placement…it is a metaphysical, emotional, and mental place as well. It is the embodiment of your relationship with the universe. To change your place, work from within, and let it manifest without.

In the majority of the magical work I currently do the focus is on embodying the magic, starting from within, or bringing the desired possibility into my space, and choosing to become it and letting it move me accordingly. Genuine transformation is the understanding that you are moved by the magic and by your own commitment to doing the necessary internal work that paves the way to the new expression of reality that expresses your connection with the universe and the space you embody.

If there's one description I'd use about Magical Identity is that it's really an exploration of magic as a transformative process. So what does that mean? When I think about western magical practices mostly what I think of is a fixation on achieving measurable results, but I think that's what missing is an exploration of transformation and the role magic can play in the transformation of your life. I'd argue that any result you achieve isn't merely a change in the external environment that happens to suit you, but is also a transformation of you as both a person and magician. That this transformation isn't considered is always a cause for concern, because it's something that shouldn't be ignored.

If we look at the anatomy of a magical act, there is a focus on change. Something needs to be changed in order to bring the world back into balance for the magician. But assuming that the change only occurs in the external environment is a mistake. The magician is also changing his/her internal reality in order to align it with the desired external result. And if they can't change the internal reality, the external result may manifest, but it won't last. At a recent talk I asked attendees how many had manifested a desired result only to have it go away without bringing the desired change they wanted. Most nodded their heads and the reason for that is simple. Their internal reality didn't align with the desired external reality they wanted.

Effective transformation calls on the magician to be in touch with their internal reality so that they can truly determine if a desired result is in alignment with their life. The magical act is a transformation of the life of the magician as well as the environment. The two aren't separate, and whatever separation we assign is a convenient illusion used to avoid understanding the act of transformation.

This doesn't mean magic involves the law of attraction or other newagey concepts. Rather what it means is that achieving a result involves a level of internal work that complements any external work that is done to achieve the result. The recognition that magic is a transformative process is a recognition that a given magical act occurs on an ontological level and involves a recognition of embodiment as a principle for manifestation. The result you desire is something that you need to embody in your existence, or write it in your code to use a technology metaphor.

Transformation, as a principle of magic, is the recognition that changing reality involves a fundamental shift that occurs on every level of your being. In other words, you recognize that a desired result is really a change occurring within and around you. But it goes beyond even that. Transformation is a change in reality itself. It's a changing of your relationship with reality. In a way I view transformation as a change in your space and in your time. I treat space and time as separate elements in this description because they are not one and the same. Your space is much more permanent than your time might be. Time changes. It's action, its flow, its movement. Space is grounding, identification, where you are, while time is presence becoming. More on that in a different correspondence course.

Transformation changes your relationship with the universe, to the extent that the change is meaningfully made to your life. It's not that you change the entire universe, but rather that you transform your place in it as well as what you attract in your life. However even that level of transformation is profound and appreciating its role in magical work can help you understand the full extent to which magic works in your life. *Undertaking a magical working is a transformation of your life.* Even your daily work is a reflection of that idea. The daily work you do ideally does has a cumulative effect on your discipline, but also on your discovery of who you are.

Transformation is the conscious choice to change yourself as a result of doing magic. This means you are fully prepared and willing to take on your transformation as a person into who you really want to be. This is significant because when we use magic we are changing more than the environment around us. We are changing our place in the universe. I can't emphasize that enough because when it is fully considered it causes you to recognize how important it is to utilize magic responsibly. It's never just a matter of solving a problem or getting that person you want. It's a matter of you becoming who you are through that act of magic and recognizing how you also impact the ontological existence of others in a very real way.

This isn't to say you shouldn't do magical work for a specific desire, but rather that you be very certain you want that desire and can handle the ramifications of achieving it in both your environment, and how you identify yourself. That kind of consideration can save you a lot of grief and trouble. I know that

I do less overt acts of magic these days in part because I have found a degree of satisfaction and contentedness with my life. Nonetheless I am still active in some ways as I work to continue transform my life as well as my environment. All of the work done is from an ontological perspective...not merely doing, but focusing instead on being. It is an exploration of identity via magical work.

When I think about magic and identity, I think about embodiment and being. In particular with the word being, I think of it as a verb that denotes a person's life as a process of presence entering into collaboration with reality. The presence of a person contains all the potential of the person, as well as access to possibilities of what the person can become. Magic, when employed, is a melding of the identity of the person (their being) with the situation. It is presence joining reality, merging possibility with what already is to create something which nonetheless contains the presence/being of the magician.

When we no longer divorce our actions from our state of being what we find is a different awareness of possibility and magic. No longer is a problem looked at as something external and separate, but instead there is an acknowledgement of the connection between the magician and the problem. The magician examines not merely the problem as it shows up in the world around them, but also the problem as it shows up in themselves, to understand the connection it has to their life, and also to understand how to solve it, not merely in the environment around them, but also within.

When being is a verb there is a recognition that ontology is not some static image of identity, but an active presence of identity that challenges the magician to know him/herself as a fluid reality that mixes with possibility on a regular basis. We are all gates to possibility, and thus our state of being is one of change. Identity, when perceived this way, is not about attachments but about becoming and unbecoming all at once. Magic is a process of identity, part of the becoming and unbecoming, simultaneously binding us to possibilities while undoing connections to others. Reality itself is no longer perceived as static, so much as it is a canvas to be painted on. What seems real falls away as possibilities are embodied in everyday life. What becomes real is a melding of presence and reality and as such it can become unreal under the right circumstances.

Magical practice based on an ontological approach frees the magician from a doing and having perspective which tends to cause the magician to objectify reality and even themselves. To have something is to own it and possess it, and yet it also possesses you. To do something is to act on it and yet try and separate yourself from it, ignoring that it has its own influence on you. Such perspectives limit the magician and dull the mind. The ontological approach acknowledges that everything is connected and that what is acted on, also acts on the magician. There is no objectification of reality, but instead a profound realization of connection and understanding that any situation encountered by the magician has a connection that goes deeper than what casual observation displays. And when the magician can make changes to their presence, the core of their own reality, they also makes changes to reality around them, changing the ontological state of not only themselves but also reality as they understand it.

Transformation isn't the change of a situation, but the change in your state of being as a result of combining the reality you are in with the possibility of a reality you wish to embody. The situation changes because the magician transforms their relationship with that situation and with the world around themselves. As such it is not so important that the situation so much as it is that the magician changes and is able to, in the process into what they desires.

It's worth noting that genuine transformation is motivated by desire. Whether it's a desire for a better life or the person you see across the way or something else, your desire fuels the transformation of who you are into who you could be, as well as what the world could offer you. As such it's important to respect desire as a motivator and mover of transformation. At the same time you don't want to be ruled by your desires to the point that it becomes an addiction. While an addiction is a transformation, it a transformation to a loss of control, respect, and discipline. Conscious transformation is our goal and to achieve conscious transformation we must work with our desires on a conscious level, acknowledging them, working with them, but never letting them dictate our life, so much as we choose how to dictate our lives. That is the power of the magician.

The Process of Magic Lesson 26: The Role of the Mundane

Before we wrap this book up there is one last element of the process of magic to consider. That element is the role of mundane actions in your magical process. A mundane action is an action that is done without utilizing magic. Or to put it a different way, it's an action that can be done and doesn't involve any overt magical ritual or work, in order for it to be done. I include mundane actions in the process of magic, because in my opinion they play an integral role in the realization of practical magical work. I see a mundane action as creating the path of least resistance for magical work to occur on. Additionally I'd argue that mundane activities are necessary for magic to work, or if not necessary, they make the manifestation of a possibility a lot easier than it could be.

Let's use job hunting as an example. If you JUST do magic to get a job, it's probably going to take a lot of magical energy to shift the desired possibility into reality, especially if you've done nothing else. The reason is simple. You haven't created a path of least resistance for the job to manifest. If there is a lot of resistance then you need more energy than the resistance you are encountering and to be honest, you probably won't pull it off because the resistance you are facing involves every other person applying for the job you want, as well as the availability of said job and even the desired qualifications for the job. And that's just a few factors.

But when we add mundane actions to the job hunt what we get is something different. We create a path of least resistance for the desired result to manifest. Thus going out and filling applications out or sending resumes or going to job interviews or writing thank notes contributes to your magical working by providing a path of least resistance. That path of least resistance makes it easier for your magical working to manifest. It uses the circumstances in your life to pave the way for your desired result. Mundane actions lower the amount of resistance you encounter and create a momentum that can shift the favor of the universe in your direction, instead of against you.

In fact, mundane actions can actually build up the magical energy of your job hunting magic (or any other magical work you are doing). You aren't just lowering the resistance you are encountering, but you are also building the energy up that will help you overcome that resistance and manifest the job you've been looking for. And that applies to any magical work you do. The mundane actions demonstrate the universe that you are willing and able to take on the responsibility of what you want to manifest. For that matter they also indicate your willingness, to yourself, to follow through on making your desired possibility into a reality.

Your magical process then should account for the mundane actions that you do to help manifest your desired reality. Specifically your mundane actions your feed your magical actions. When your mundane actions feed your magical actions, you give your magical work more oomph, and you manifest what you need a lot quicker as well. It surprises me how many magicians don't connect their mundane actions to their magical efforts, at least in terms of fueling the magical work you are doing. Mundane actions that are directed toward achieving a specific result that you are also doing magic for carry with them a sympathetic resonance that a magician should always capitalize on.

You shouldn't stick with the obvious mundane actions either. While filling out an application or sending a resume in is definitely an action you want to do when job hunting, you might also take the time to write out a list of what your ideal workplace is, who you want to work with, what kind of boss you want to have, etc. Beside the fact that this information will help you get very specific in your magical work, it'll also help you realize what's really important with your job search.

But a job search is just one mundane example. You can apply what I wrote above to finding a lover, or to owning a business or to dealing with a problem in your life. Some of your mundane actions won't be the same as the in the example I used above, but the point is that you actively integrate those activities into your magical work. I recommend as a first step that you figure out what mundane activities will help you with your magical work.

For instance, if you were doing magical work for your business, one mundane activity you'd definitely want to do would be to write a business plan (if one wasn't already written) or revise your existing one. You might take classes, go to networking meetings, and do a variety of other mundane activities, all of which would be used to help your magical work along. The one caveat is that you need to make sure that you can see a clear connection between the mundane action and the magical work you are doing. If there isn't a clear connection, then the mundane action isn't contributing to your magical work and shouldn't be considered in your magical process.

If you are looking for a lover in your life, you might list all the desired attributes of the person you were looking for, as well as go and do activities where you'd meet someone that you'd like to forge an intimate connection with. That mundane behavior would contribute greatly to the success of your magical working because it emphasizes what you are trying to accomplish. Magic works much better when you create a path of least resistance.

With that said, you don't always need to rely on mundane actions to successfully work magic. While, in some cases, some type of mundane action is needed to help your magical work along, sometimes they aren't needed, at least not to the extent that you'd think. As a personal example, I did a magical work to bring a magical partner into my life. I didn't find her at a local meetup or magical gathering. I actually met her at a pagan convention in California, which isn't in the same state I reside in. Obviously going to the convention helped, but beyond that there wasn't much in the way of mundane actions I performed. Everything else was magical.

Don't rule mundane actions out, but don't rely strictly on them either. The whole point of doing magical work is that you are choosing to employ resources and a process that can get things done because what's happening in your everyday life just isn't working. So use mundane actions as part of your magical process, but use them for what they are: as a way of helping you achieve your desire result in conjunction with magical work you are doing.

Exercise

The Final project for this class involves you describing what your process of magic is. How do all the lessons tie into your understanding of your magical work? What is your process of magic? What is your definition of magic and how does your magical activities (and mundane actions) create that process of magic? Do you even feel that magic is a process and why or why not? Identify each component of your magical working. How does all of it fit into your magical process? How does a process approach help you understand this working magical working and magic in general?

Conclusion

When I first created the process of Magic, I did it because I wanted to present an alternative approach to exploring how magic works, without spells and unnecessary esoteric jargon. I wanted to present the concepts and practices of magic in everyday language. At the same time I also wanted to present it in a way where a reader could take what I shared and immediately apply it to their magical practice. Hopefully I've achieved that with this book.

This is the most "basic" book on magic I'll ever write, but I hesitate to all this book a 101 book because unlike so many 101 books that are out there, its focus is on exploring and explain how magic works and introducing you to the fundamental mechanics of magic. When I offered this content as a course I had people take it who had practiced magic for years and got a lot from it, so it's not just a book for beginners, but really for anyone who wants to understand how magic works and what they can change about their understanding and practice of magic to get better results.

I've also included a couple of appendices of bonus material that goes hand in hand with the original content presented in this book. My hope is that this book will help you become a better magician.

Taylor Ellwood

Taylor Ellwood

May 2018

Portland Oregon

Appendix 1: The 7 Principles of Magical Tools

Magical tools play an important role in magical work and while you can certainly use the standard assortment of magical tools that you can find in your average occult shop, you can also create your own. Whether you buy a tool or create it, there are 7 principles of magical tools to keep in mind that can help you get the most out of your magical tools.

The first principles is that there are 2 types of magical tools. The first type is Passive and the second type is active. Passive tools (such as a figurine or statue) embody a connection to the spirit and are always on. Active tools (such as a wand) have a physical use and are activated when you use them, but otherwise are dormant. You use passive tools to keep a connection going or to honor a spirit. You use active tools to work your magic and take specific actions to get specific results.

The second principle is that the magical tool isn't just a tool in the physical sense of the world, but also a symbolic/spiritual tool. A magical tool mediates (represents and connect with) a specific force. For example, the Time Turner in Harry Potter mediates non-linear time. Any tool you work with has a specific purpose of mediating the energy/force you want to connect with. It's important to recognize and respect that aspect of tools.

The third principle acknowledges that if we work with a tool long enough, we can actually embody and mediate the force the tool represents. For instance if you continually work with the time turner in Harry Potter, it will change your perspective of time and you'll find that you don't need the tool as much, or at all, because you approach time using the experiences you've had with the tool.

The fourth principles recognizes that a tool engages your physical senses in order to connect with your spiritual senses/awareness. What this means is that your physical interactions with the tool open your spiritual awareness to the tool's symbolic and spiritual functions. When you hold an athame in your hand, the physical sensation of it plays a role in how you connect with the athame and the spiritual forces it embodies and mediates. The same is true with any other tool you work with.

The fifth principle understands that mediation allows us to make meaning that helps us understand the spiritual forces we want to work with. It also helps us understand that we work with tools in order to help us making meaning and understand how to apply that meaning to our lives, practically and metaphysically. Mediation is the embodiment of the spiritual force you are working with, and at the same time it allows you to bring that force into your life and make changes with it.

The sixth principle helps us realize that tools allow us to change our identity. This is important because if we want to create a new reality, part of what we must do is reshape our identity to fit that reality. Your magical tools help you take on the new identity and allow you to fully integrate into the new reality you've created.

The final principle recognizes that tools can be used to automate magical workings. For example, one of the tools I create is an evocation portal. The evocation portal allows me to automatically evoke the spirit it's connected with. Instead of having to do elaborate workings, I simply activate the evocation portal and we get to work. The purpose of a tool is to make what you do easier to do, so if you're going to work with a tool, why not set it up so it can perform the function its need to automatically?

All seven of these principles can help you use your magical tools more effectively and create specialized ones for specific purposes.

Appendix 2: Why you aren't getting the results you want?

Sometimes you do a magical working and you don't get the result you want. You may even think you haven't gotten a result at all. Actually, you always a gest a result, even if the result is that nothing happened. But what needs to be understood about all results, successful or unsuccessful, is that they are signs of what is or isn't working with your magical process. When you understand that about results, then you can learn from them.

I added this appendix because I want to help you understand why you are or aren't getting the results you want, as well as provide you some ideas on what you can change to start getting better results. The problems I list below are common problems I see that stops magicians from getting results.

Problem 1: You aren't defining your results

The number one problem I usually see other magicians have is that they don't do a good job of defining the desired result. They worry that if they define the result and are specific it will make it harder to manifest that results.

But if anything, I've found that when you get specific about your desired result, it becomes much easier to manifest it.

Why?

Well a vague result leaves a lot open for interpretation. For example let's say you decide to do magic to get a job. If your desired result is simply to get a job, than any old job will do. Your result isn't very specific.

So how do you define a result that you want? There's a 2 step process that's involved...

First you need to define what you DON'T want. In the case of a job this includes being specific about what work you don't want to do, but also the types of people you don't want to work with.

Second you want to define what you DO want. This includes defining the type of work and people you want to work with, but also how much money you want t make, and benefits.

Now that is getting incredibly specific and the benefit of that specificity is that when you do your magical working, you focus it on the target that you want. This focuses your activities and behaviors as well toward helping you achieve the desired result.

And by defining what you don't want, as well as what you want, you get clear on the result that will actually make a difference, instead of just settling for any result.

Problem 2: Some part of you is resistant to getting the result

It may be hard to believe, but sometimes we don't really want the results we say we want...or at least part of us doesn't.

The problem with internal resistance to a result is that it sabotages the result. Even if you get a result for the short term that part of you that is resistant will find some way to undermine you, and the result will go away.

There are different reasons why we feel internal resistance. Let's explore what those are.

The first reason you may feel internal resistance toward a result could be that the result (or the way you achieved it) goes against your ethical/moral code. If you ever have part of yourself screaming don't do something in your mind, it's wise to heed that voice and figure out why some part of you feels resistant.

However you could be honoring your ethical/moral compass and still sabotage the result. In that case, it could be that part of you feels unworthy of the result. When we don't feel worthy of something, we find a way to get rid of it, because that lack of worthiness makes us feel uncomfortable with ourselves. Until you work through your feelings of unworthiness, those feelings will top you from getting the results you want.

Finally you might just come to the conclusion that you didn't want the result that you thought you wanted. Sometimes having something manifest makes you realize you don't really need it. In such a case, it's a good idea to do some thinking on why you felt it was important and what changed.

So how do you resolve the internal resistance?

In the case of your ethical/moral compass, it's important to honor your code and stick to it. If you can't find a way to achieve a result that doesn't violate that code, you either need to change your code, or abandon the result.

In the case of not feeling worthy, you need to figure out what the underlying beliefs and narratives are about your unworthiness. I recommend doing some type of meditation that allows you to sit with and work through the emotions around your feeling of unworthiness.

Problem 3: I didn't get the result immediately

Some people do a magical working and expect the result to manifest immediately. The problem is they've bought into the Hollywood version of magic that seems to work spontaneously. But what we practice isn't Hollywood magic and while it is possible to get a result to manifest shortly after you've done a ritual, not all results will occur that quickly and sometimes you may not want them to.

It really comes down to understanding the role of timing in magic. A good question to ask is when do I want the result to manifest (and possibly where)? Getting a result immediately may not always be the best possible outcome, because it may not afford you the opportunity to fully take advantage of it.

Some of the best results I've gotten with magic has involved setting the working up around when I want the result to show up.

So how do you go about doing that?

First you need to recognize that time is always a variable and that you can purposely apply that variable to your working and second you need to ask yourself when you need that result.

Then program that desired time into your working and let it happen.

What many people forget is that magic isn't a cure all or instant gratification. It's the alignment of the right variables that stack the deck of fate in your favor and help you turn a desired possibility into a reality.

Problem 4: You don't recognize the result

Sometimes we don't recognize the result, because we're so busy looking for it to show up in a way that we expect that we don't open ourselves to unexpected avenues of manifestation.

It's also worth remembering that magic often operates in a very subtle way.

When it seems like you haven't achieved your result, consider first what would tell you if you'd accomplished your result. Then consider if perhaps your limiting yourself to only seeing the result if it showed up in that way.

Finally consider what other ways the result might show up and start exploring if it has shown up in a way you didn't expect.

What makes magic, well magic is that it doesn't always operate in the way we expect. We can do a magical working and send the magic out into the world and have it come back in a way we don't plan for, which is nonetheless valid.

Problem 5: You aren't keep a record of your work

It's hard to keep track of what's working or not working if you have no records. An objective record allows you to find what is or isn't working. It takes what's in your head and puts it in a place you can see it. If you aren't getting the results you want, start keeping track of what you are and aren't doing as well as any other variables that stand out to you. Looking over this information can help you figure out what is or isn't working.

I also recommend keeping a record so that you can improve on your magical workings. Tracing what you've done and what results you've gotten can help you figure out what you want to change in your magical workings as well as how to improve your process.

Problem 6: Inconsistent magical practice

One reason people don't get results is because they have an inconsistent magical practice. They only practice magic when they need something or have a problem come up, or for a holiday. Otherwise magic is just tossed to the side and forgotten about.

Magic, like exercise requires consistency if you want to get consistent results. Inconsistent practice makes it harder because you aren't operating at your optimal. If you lack the discipline to practice magic consistently then it should be no surprise when you don't get results. Once you make magic a consistent part of your life, you'll notice changes in your practice because of the consistency.

I need your help!

Thanks for reading The Process of Magic. If you found *The Process of Magic* helpful to you I would really appreciate it if you would leave a review on Goodreads.com, Amazon.com and other book sites where you purchase books.

If you email me a link with your published review for *The Process of Magic* I'll send you a review copy of my book *Space/Time Magic Foundations*. It's all about how to develop your own space/time magic workings and I've included the first chapter as a bonus in this books.

About the Author

Taylor Ellwood is the author of numerous books on magic including Pop Culture Magick, Space/Time Magic, and Inner Alchemy. When he isn't working on his latest magical experiment or writing a book he can be found enjoying games, books, and life. For more information about his latest projects, check out his site http://www.magicalexperiments.com

Get a Sneak Peak of Space/Time Magic Foundations!

Also Available Magical Experiments Press

Lesson 1: What is Space/Time Magic and Why is it Important for Magical Work?

Look at the question above. The answer may seem obvious to you. Or it may not be obvious at all. Regardless, the reason we start this course with this question is to provide a foundation upon which to build our later work, both in this course, and for the in person classes. Defining what magic is, or what a type of magic is, provides the magician an essential understanding of what s/he is doing and why s/he is doing it. This understanding informs the process of magic, and how magic shows up in our lives.

What is Space/Time Magic?

Space/time magic is magic that is focused on working with the elements of space and time, as well as other elements that are relevant to the first two. It is also magic that is focused on manifesting possibilities into reality and turning imagination into manifestation. Space/time magic works with the past, present, and future as well as alternate variations of a person's life. Space/time magic is also one of the evolutions of magic as a discipline. A space/time magician isn't caught up in the usual formula and ceremony of more traditional practices of magic, but instead is interested in evolving magic into a contemporary discipline that has relevance with what we, as human beings, deal with every day.

In the next two lessons we will explore the elements of space and time at some depth, but in order to define space/time magic, I want to briefly define these elements, and also explore the other elements which are relevant to our practice of space/time magic. What I provide here is not the end all, be all of space/time magic, but rather is a description of what it can be. Ultimately it is on you to decide what space/time magic is or isn't. I'm a guide who can help you make discoveries, but you are the final judge of your journey into this discipline.

Space: Space is everywhere. Space is formless and yet is defined by forms. It is formless in the sense that it exists regardless of what forms are in it, but it is defined by the forms that exist within it, to the extent that those forms provide context for your interaction with space. Space is a place that roots you in reality, but also exposes you to the possibilities that are inherent to space.

Time: Time is a perception we use to make sense of the rhythms of life. Time measures and orders the rhythms of life, the events we experience, and even how we measure distance and the passage of our lives. Time is linear and non-linear, dependent on your perception of it and your willingness to experiment with it. Time is action that changes space, and moves you from one identity to another.

Stillness: Stillness is the experience of presence, of being in the moment. Yet conversely stillness is also the experience of possibility. When we are still we open ourselves to the moment as it is, and at the same time we also open ourselves to the possibilities that are available in the moment. Stillness teaches us that existing in the moment is just as valuable as focusing on the future or past and that we can use that choice of stillness to discover opportunity, because we are taking the moment to really be still instead of trying to change everything. Change starts from within and stillness teaches us to become that initial change that we want to bring to our lives.

Movement: Movement is action. When we think of movement, we likely think of physical movement, but movement can also be emotional, mental, and spiritual. Movement, in space/time magic is the choice to manifest a possibility into reality. We discover the possibility we manifest and we move it into reality through our actions, thoughts, and choices. Until we move, a possibility is just potential waiting to happen. Once we move possibility becomes reality because we are taking the necessary actions to turn possibility into some real. I also think of movement as a form of embodiment and identity. When you physically move your body, you carry your identity with that movement. The same applies to movements we apply to manifesting a possibility into reality. We are embodying the possibility and making it an integral part of our identity, as a way of establishing it as reality.

Imagination/Memory: Imagination and memory are really one and the same. We use memory to "remember" or imagine the past and we use imagination to imagine or "remember" the future. We'll call memory imagination from now on, in order to simplify the terms we are using. Imagination allows us to comprehend and connect with possibilities. It allows us to manipulate space and time, as well as a variety of other elements we experience and work with, including magic. Imagination is one of the more important and powerful magical tools we have, and learning how to work with it is important for working with space and time.

Possibility: A possibility is an unrealized reality that can only become realized when you take the requisite steps to make it "real." Some possibilities are easier to manifest than others due to two factors. The first factor is probability, specifically how likely it is the possibility would manifest as a reality without anyone's help. The second factor is imagination, specifically the ability to imagine the possibility as a reality. The more improbable it is to your imagination that a possibility could be real, the harder it is to manifest it. It should also be noted that possibilities don't stay at a fixed value of probability. A possibility can become more or less probable due to the actions of other people, events, etc., as well as what consensual reality dictates. If consensual reality is treated as something which is fixed, it actually makes possibilities harder to manifest because the collective imagination of people hold onto a rigid set of principles that dictate how reality should behave.

Reality: Reality is an illusion, albeit a consensual illusion. Essentially what we think of as real is only "real" because we agree that it's real. The reason you don't see a person flying in the air partially is due to gravity, but also because we can't really conceive of a reality where a person could fly (on their own power). The closest we come to is via comic books and fantasy stories and even then it's usually attributed to some outside force or something that is unique to the character. We can change reality, and magic is one way we can change it, but if you think about how magic works, it tends to be a lot less splashy and visible, and much more subtle. It works because the focus is on aligning possibility with reality, but even what works is shaped in part by consensual reality and what we know about the principles that govern reality. The more malleable reality becomes, the easier it is to manifest more improbable possibilities into reality. What keeps reality locked in place has more to do with the consensual beliefs that people hold about reality that anything else, in my opinion. Your mileage may vary, and there's no "proof" that I'm right but consider that the very need for proof is an example of how consensual reality is sustained and maintained in order to establish a status quo.

Identity: Your identity is the agreement you've made with the universe, which sets up the various experiences you'll have. Your identity isn't set in stone, but is something that can be continually changed through your choices. We usually only pay attention to major changes to identity such as marriage or a birthday, but your identity changes on a daily basis. For example if you are hungry, that's an identity, which is changed once you eat. It's not a major change, but it nonetheless can change your behavior and experience of the day. Your identity des establish a pattern to your reality and what you experience and if you want to change what you are experiencing you may need to change those patterns. For example if you find that you are consistently getting rejected by people you are interested in, you need to examine your identity around that issue. Are you getting rejected because of certain behaviors or certain limiting beliefs you hold about yourself? Are you picking people that you know will reject you because you don't believe you can do any better? By examining your identity as it applies to situations you encounter, you can make changes to your identity by changing the underlying values and beliefs that support those situations. And that is actually an integral part of my own approach to space/time magic.

Why is Space/Time Magic important for magical work?

Having looked at the various elements that can apply to space/time magic, it's also important to understand why space/time magic is important to magical work. The first reason space/time magic is important is based on history, namely that it's been for longer than we might think. Your typical occultist might assume that space/time magic start with chaos magic and Peter Carroll's experimentation with it, but if anything space/time magic has been around since at least the beginning of the twentieth century and perhaps even longer.

In fact, I'd go so far as to argue that space/time magic has been around since at least Ancient Greece, where the rhetoricians of the time experimented with developing a memory technique that would allow them to recall a long speech using symbolism to store the information of the speech in a virtual environment (usually a temple) where the rhetorician would imagine the symbols within a specific sequential order that they'd then use to recall the contents of the speech. And perhaps it's been around for as long as we've been able to perceive space and time. Regardless space/time magic isn't necessarily a new discipline. Even if we rule out the rhetoricians of ancient Greece, we will find that there has been some work with space/time magic since the early Twentieth Century.

Julius Evola, an Italian magician wrote about his own experiments with Space/Time magic in the UR journal, which was a collection of articles written in the 1930's. William Gray wrote about Space/Time Magic in the 1960's and R. J. Stewart has been writing about the topic since he first started writing in the 1970's. Peter Carroll and Phil Hine and other magicians have written about the topic, contributing a variety of ideas and techniques all oriented around space, time, and magic. Space/Time Magic has steadily become more prevalent as humanity has made space/time more relevant to their own experience of life. However a historical basis is just one of the reasons space/time magic is important to our magical practices.

Another reason is the cultural relevance that space and time have come to occupy in our collective consciousness. Our watches and phones are physical artifacts that represent time, and our fixation on knowing what time it is, is one example of this cultural relevance. And knowing what time it is, is important because we schedule the space of that time with meetings, or go to specific spaces that have specific meanings to us.

Different cultures have different experiences of time, which is based in part on the priority assigned to time, but also how time is used to define space as well as how space defines time. To some degree, every person you meet is conscious of time and space at any given moment, and uses that awareness to define their own sense of reality and sense of place in the world. This relevance is taken for granted by most people because we live with it all the time, and yet I think a conscious awareness of space and time, in and of themselves is useful as a form of magic because it can provide us a variety of opportunities to explore the deliberate manipulation of space and time.

Science and its exploration of space/time also needs to be noted. Magicians such as Peter Carroll have attempted to apply scientific understandings of space/time to magical practice. Then there's the scientific work in and of itself which has some useful information to provide about space/time. I'll admit that the focus of my own work in space/time magic doesn't draw on the science as much, because I'm more interested in how space/time can be explored through non-scientific explanations.

Nevertheless every space/time magician I know (myself included) is influenced to some degree by the science.

Space/time magic is relevant to magical work because it is part of the continual evolution of magic as a discipline. For magic to continue to be relevant in our lives and in the future, it must evolve as a discipline. So many of the classical and traditional approaches to magic are weighed down by a tendency to value what is old over what is new. It's a rather romantic perspective of the past, which ignores the simple fact that what makes magic relevant in our lives isn't what our ancestors experienced or worshipped, but rather what we ourselves are experiencing. For some Pagans and magicians there is a need to draw on the past because it provides a sense of place. But I don't think we should draw on the past exclusively. Rather we must face what is around us and use that as well to chart a path for further magical exploration.

My own interests in space/time magic began in the late 90's when I began experimenting with them as elements that were (and are) relevant to my life. My work with space/time magic has continually moved in that direction and I would guess that if you are taking this class it's because you recognize that space/time are relevant to you. Now the question is how is it relevant?

Discussion topic: What were your first experiences with space/time magic? How did space/time become relevant to you as a magician and how are you currently working with space/time in your magical practice. If you aren't working with space/time as elements of magic, how would you like to work with them?

CPSIA information can be obtained
at www.ICGtesting.com
Printed in the USA
LVHW050007050520
654936LV00008B/2374

9 781720 827306